PEOPLE IN SCIENCE

Earth and the Environment

Peter Ellis

Pearson Education
Edinburgh Gate
Harlow
Essex
CM20 2JE
www.peopleinscience.co.uk

Immersive Education
The Old Malthouse
Paradise Street
Oxford
OX1 1LD

ISBN 0582 773091

Design concept by Raven Design, Ware, Herts
and Gemini Design, Hersham, Surrey
Page make-up by Gemini Design, Hersham, Surrey
Cover and CD label design by Immersive Education Limited
Reprinted by Pear Tree Press Ltd, Stevenage Herts SG1 2BH

The publisher's policy is to use paper manufactured from sustainable forests.

Acknowledgments
The Immersive Education team are: Alex Cane; Ashfaq Khan; Ben Hanke; Boris Samson; Brian Unwin; Carol Macintosh; Claire James; Damien Rochford; David Hailey; Donna Burton–Wilcock; Ian Downend; James Broad; John McDonnell; Lloyd Sutton; Marie-Claire Barnes; Simon Beaumont; Stephen Hawkins; Steve Young; Rebecca Benbow; Vicky Carroll; John Griffiths; Ashley Helm; Sarah Hickman; Steven Howell; Zoe Klinger; Andy Krouwel; Chris Lloyd; Tim Price-Walker; Michael Reading; Diane Rees; Stephanie Rogers; Theresa Rose; Ray Shaw; Jamie Sheldon; Ross Walker; Martin Weatherill; David Welch; Chris Wild; Jeff Woyda.

Peter Ellis has been teaching science for 27 years and has an M.Phil in Chemical Education. He served a term as Chairman of the Education Section of the British Society for the History of Science.

Alastair Sandiforth is Head of Science at Stanborough School, Welwyn Garden City. He is also a Principal Examiner for GCSE Biology and Assistant Principal Moderator for GCSE Science coursework.

We are grateful to the following for permission to reproduce photographs:
Limestone image, Science Photo Library; Granite and Slate images, GeoScience Features Picture Library.

PEOPLE IN SCIENCE

Earth and the Environment

Peter Ellis

kar2ouche®

Contents

A Introduction

People in Science – Earth and the Environment is one of a series of six CD-ROMs each with accompanying support materials. They are designed to help teachers deliver the Ideas and Evidence strand of Sc1 in an interesting and motivating manner, and to develop students' thinking and literacy skills at the same time. The series is accompanied by a companion website at **www.peopleinscience.co.uk**.

Kar2ouche®

People in Science uses Kar2ouche® – an innovative software product that allows students to read and/or listen to text, and to create storyboards describing a sequence of events, or present arguments, debates, or factual information. Suggestions for different ways of using Kar2ouche® to teach science and to develop thinking and literacy skills are given in Sections B and C (pages 8–11). A 'Quick-Start' guide to using Kar2ouche® is provided at the back of this file, and a full instruction manual can be downloaded from the website at **www.peopleinscience.co.uk**.

Ideas about the Earth and the Environment

Earth and the Environment covers two areas which have recently undergone rapid changes in scientific theory. The first set of activities looks at our understanding of the Earth itself. Wegener's ideas are discussed and built upon to give us the modern picture of the Earth and the rock cycle. Modern characters then discuss the problem of predicting changes in the Earth's crust, such as earthquakes and volcanos. The second set of activities looks at two of the environmental problems which are facing the world, namely global warming and the hole in the ozone layer. Each problem is looked at from a historical point of view, as well as asking pupils to look at possible solutions. An outline of the scientific developments covered by *Earth and the Environment* is given in section D (page 12), and short biographies of the characters are included in Section E (page 17).

Section F (page 21) provides matching charts to map the themes to:
- the National Curriculum for England
- the National Curriculum for Wales
- the Guidelines for Scotland
- Scottish Standard Grade specifications.

In addition, matching charts are available on the website for the following:
- the QCA Scheme of Work for England
- GCSE specifications from AQA, Edexcel and OCR
- National Literacy Strategy.

The Themes

The material provided on this CD can be used to cover a number of themes; either specific discoveries or ideas (e.g. plate tectonics) or ways of doing science (e.g. the importance of evidence in the development of ideas). This pack includes 6 suggested Themes, covering different aspects of ideas about the Earth and the Environment. For each Theme there are two suggested activities (of varying difficulty), a set of Teacher's Notes, a classwork sheet and a homework sheet. The CD includes two partially completed storyboards for each theme, to help students to get started on the activities.

5

The activities and storyboards

In writing the activities we have attempted to provide a variety of tasks as well as looking at different scientific ideas. The suggested activities vary from creating straightforward storyboards to describe a sequence of events, to constructing a photostory and a newspaper article. We have provided two activities for each Theme, with the first activity generally being easier than the second. The suitability of each activity for KS3 and KS4 pupils is indicated in the Teacher's Notes. Each activity is further differentiated into Sections A, B and C. Students should all start on section A.

A storyboard is provided for each activity (except for Activity 1.1C for which a Word template is provided instead). These storyboards can be accessed from the text/audio window (click the blue book symbol). The storyboards have some frames already created, and prompts or questions in the comment window below the frame. The classwork sheets provided give students a brief outline of the activity and suggestions for completing the storyboard.

The activities suggested in this pack are intended to help teachers and students new to working with Kar2ouche® – there are many other possible activities and themes that can be covered using the text and characters provided. A few more suggestions are given in Section H (page 57).

Kar2ouche® allows teachers to personalise various settings, determining which characters, backgrounds and props students have access to. Further details on this facility can be found in the user manual.

The Homework Sheets

A homework sheet is provided for every Theme. The sheets are intended to be 'stand-alone', in that they do not rely on students having completed all of the corresponding activity, and they do not require students to take home printed versions of their classwork activities. They are intended to consolidate ideas introduced via the activities.

We have provided a range of questions to be used on each homework sheet. Teachers may like to select which questions students are to use for homework depending on the ability of the class.

One question on each sheet is a research question highlighted by the following icon: 🔍 . These require students to use books or the Internet. Suggested weblinks are given on the *People in Science* website at **www.peopleinscience.co.uk**. or in the Teacher's Notes where appropriate.

The Teacher's Notes

The Teacher's Notes for each Theme include the following information:

Activity	KS3	KS4
1.1	Most	All
1.2	Some	Most

a box indicating which students the activities are suitable for. 'All' means that all students at that Key Stage should be capable of carrying out the activity successfully; 'Most' means that most students should be able to carry out the activity, but that it is not suitable for the least able (or the least able will need considerable help); and 'Some' indicates that the activity is suitable for more able students only at that Key Stage.

➡ learning objectives

➡ learning outcomes

➡ an indication of any prior knowledge that students will need before starting the activities

➡ a list of National Curriculum statements that can be covered (or partially covered) using the activities

➡ a brief background summary of the scientific developments or debates covered by the Theme

➡ an outline of the suggested activities and the storyboards provided

➡ a list of the characters, backgrounds and props needed (this provides a quick reference list in case teachers wish to lock out any characters, props or backgrounds not needed for the activities)

➡ suggestions for organising the lesson

➡ answers to questions on the homework sheet.

The website www.peopleinscience.co.uk

The companion website includes:

➡ a full user manual for Kar2ouche®, downloadable as pdf files

➡ Frequently Asked Questions

➡ an area where teachers can submit or download ideas or storyboards, to share teaching ideas with other schools

➡ a list of weblinks suitable for answering the research questions for each Theme.

At the time of publication, all web addresses listed in the Teacher's File have been checked for their content and suitability. However, we would advise that all weblinks are tested before use in class, to ensure that they are still useful and appropriate. Any updates needed to the web addresses will be posted on the *People in Science* website.

Customer Support

Kar2ouche® is easy to install and run, but if problems are encountered, call the Customer Support Line on 01865 811001.

System Requirements	PC/Windows System Requirements	Mac OS System Requirements
• 50 Mb free hard drive space • 32 Mb of RAM • CD-ROM drive • Mouse • 1024 x 768 or 800 x 600 16-bit video display • Microphone and speakers *(Kar2ouche® will work without these, but users will not experience the benefits of the software without them.)*	• 300 MHz or higher Pentium compatible processor • Windows 95/98/2000/ME/XP • Microsoft DirectX 8.0 or higher *(installed automatically if not found)* • QuickTime 5.0 or higher *(installed automatically if not found)*	• Suitable for PowerMac or Powerbook • Mac OS 8.6 or later • CarbonLib 1.1 • QuickTime 5.0 or higher *(installed automatically if not found)*

B Using *People in Science* in the classroom

The material provided on the *People in Science* CDs can be used in the classroom in a number of ways. This section gives a general overview of the possibilities, with more detailed suggestions for each Theme given in the Teacher's Notes and via the ready-made storyboards.

Organising the lesson

Students gain most value from the kinds of activity suggested here if they are given a general introduction to the lesson before they start using the software, and if what they have learned can be summarised and shared with others during a plenary session at the end of the lesson. Specific suggestions for starting and finishing lessons are made in the Teacher's Notes for each Theme.

Students can work alone, in pairs or even threes. For many students, working in pairs provides encouragement, an opportunity to share ideas, and a chance to clarify ideas by discussion with a partner. For this reason, it may be better to ask students to work in pairs even if there are sufficient computers for students to be able to work alone.

Storyboards

A storyboard is a series of frames that tell a story or convey a sequence of events. They can be viewed as separate frames in sequence or animated and played as a 'movie'. Storyboards are particularly useful in encouraging students to show their understanding and demonstrate their ability to extract and summarise key information.

Students can be asked to create:
- ➡ a summary of a particular event or piece of text in a specified number of frames
- ➡ a summary with speech bubbles or captions containing important quotations
- ➡ a storyboard with their own commentary or a summary in their own words
- ➡ presentations for the class to view
- ➡ illustrations of alternative points of view, or a debate
- ➡ imagined meetings between characters
- ➡ a proposal for a new documentary to be presented to a board of TV executives.

While the main ideas in a storyboard are likely to be conveyed via text (either in the text window or in speech, thought or text bubbles), students can enhance their presentations by adding sound effects, extra characters or props, all of which can be found on the CD. In addition, they can add their own digital images, or record the text in their own voices.

If time is limited, teachers can provide partially completed storyboards that students finish in the lesson. Students can also be asked to create their own incomplete storyboards for other students to complete. Partially completed storyboards may comprise, for example:
- ➡ the first and last frames – students make the frames for the central section
- ➡ storyboards that contain blank thought bubbles, blank speech bubbles and/or blank text boxes
- ➡ storyboards with questions in text boxes or in the caption window
- ➡ storyboards with text in the caption window – students create the pictures
- ➡ storyboards with odd frames missing
- ➡ sequencing activities
- ➡ a quiz – 'who says what?', or 'what happens next?'

8

Animations

Students who have access to Kar2ouche® out of class time enjoy creating animations. As with storyboards, animations enable students to demonstrate their understanding and ability to extract key information. Most of the activities listed below can also be created as still storyboards. Students may be told that they have been commissioned to create a:

- a news programme
- a documentary
- a TV chat show/interview
- a documentary trailer.

Publications

To summarise a topic, students can present their storyboards to the class using a data projector, interactive whiteboard, or on screen. Alternatively, they can use the print facility to create publications in Kar2ouche®, or copy images into a word processing or desktop publishing program.

Possible publications for students to create include:

- a newspaper front page – using Kar2ouche® to compose the pictures
- storybooks – picture above, story below in text window
- cartoon strips (or film strips)
- diary entries (with photos/pictures)
- letters (with pictures)
- photo albums
- magazine spreads.

In all of these activities students may be asked to consider audience and purpose. Teachers can stipulate this audience.

The possibilities are almost endless. As teachers get used to the software and use it within their particular area of expertise, other activities will suggest themselves.

C Developing thinking and literacy skills

Although the focus of the activities in *People in Science* is for students to learn about science, in particular the development of ideas and evidence over time, there are also ample opportunities for pupils to develop their thinking skills and literacy skills. This section outlines some of the skills that can be developed. A matching chart is available on the website, which links the suggested activities to the National Literacy Strategy.

Information-processing skills

Students can be encouraged to:

- ➡ identify key images, text, and ideas – and extract what is essential
- ➡ sort the relevant from the irrelevant
- ➡ organise and, where necessary, prioritise ideas
- ➡ sequence events
- ➡ compare and contrast their work with the work of others.

Reasoning skills

Students can be encouraged to:

- ➡ justify opinions using evidence
- ➡ make informed choices
- ➡ consider alternative perspectives or interpretations
- ➡ articulate ideas.

Enquiry skills

Students can be encouraged to:

- ➡ work collaboratively to extract information from texts
- ➡ consider consequences
- ➡ reflect critically on written text, their own work and the work of their peers.

Creative thinking skills

Students can be encouraged to:

- ➡ offer interpretations of texts or situations
- ➡ create multi-media texts
- ➡ respond imaginatively to texts or situations.

Evaluation skills

Students can be encouraged to:

- ➡ engage in collaborative work and dialogue
- ➡ review, modify and evaluate work produced.

Communication

Students can be encouraged to:

- ➡ engage in group discussion
- ➡ present ideas to a group
- ➡ use visual aids and images to enhance communication
- ➡ listen, understand and respond critically to others.

Literacy skills

At **word level** you can draw attention to key scientific words and their spelling. Students should be encouraged to look up any unfamiliar words in the glossary provided on the CD, and to compile their own lists of new words. Alternatively, lists of new words can be made into posters and used in a wall display. When introducing new vocabulary, encourage students to draw on analogies to known words, roots, derivations, and familiar spelling patterns.

In creating a range of storyboards, students can be encouraged to pay attention to **sentence level** literacy skills. In particular they should pay attention to sentence structure and the consistent use of tenses. At a more advanced level they should be encouraged to consider the differences between written and spoken language in terms of degrees of formality and the techniques that speakers employ to persuade an audience to their points of view.

Work at a **text level** can be varied. As far as the students' **reading** skills are concerned the activities require them to develop a range of research and study skills, including locating information from the given text through skimming, scanning and search techniques. At a more advanced level they are required to bring in information from a range of sources, and to evaluate and re-present this for a specific audience. Some students may need clear directions that will help them to develop these skills.

The **writing** demands of the activities are varied from virtual performances and debates to newspaper reports. Students should be shown how to take effective notes, organise ideas and use evidence. If time permits, it would also be useful to reinforce literacy work by modelling some of the writing types particularly relevant to science – for instance, report writing, and where possible, to provide writing scaffolds for students who need most support.

The software is particularly suitable for pair and small group work and thus for facilitating the development of **speaking and listening** skills. When working in pairs, students can be given instructions to use talk as a tool for clarifying ideas by discussing, hypothesising, citing evidence and asking questions. In many of the activities students are required to promote, justify or defend a point of view using supporting evidence, example and illustration. During plenary sessions students will be required to listen, ask questions, comment, and possibly evaluate the presentations they have viewed. With teacher direction, students can be allocated different roles in their groups to practise different skills. The storyboarding activities allow pupils to engage in virtual role-play, therefore developing their drama techniques in a variety of situations and in response to a range of stimuli.

D The development of ideas about the Earth and the Environment

The study of rocks began when primitive humans began picking up flints to make into tools, searching for clays to make baskets waterproof, and selecting different earths to make into pigments for body painting and cave art. The ability to recognise different rocks and minerals developed further when people began to use metals, and up to the end of the medieval period miners were the most knowledgeable about the rocks beneath our feet.

During the eighteenth century, there were other reasons for needing to know the identities and properties of the rocks below the soil, such as building canals. William Smith produced the first geological map of Britain in 1815, and was amongst the first to recognise that rocks could be classified and identified by the fossils in them. Also during the eighteenth century, the fashion for collecting took in rocks and fossils as well as plants and animals, and there was a growing interest in the shape of the land.

Theories about the origins of the rocks and the shape of the Earth itself were slow to develop. Aristotle believed the Earth to be eternal but its surface subject to processes which produced cycles of change. European scholars in the Christian era had faith in the creation stories in the Bible. This led Archbishop James Ussher, in 1650, to calculate that the Earth had been created in 4004 BCE. However, even at this time, some philosophers were beginning to doubt that the Genesis stories could be taken literally. The stage was set for the coming of age of the science of geology, and for theories of the origins of rocks.

Different theories

Towards the end of the eighteenth century two opposing views about the origins of rocks emerged, championed by contrasting characters. Abraham Gottlob Werner, born in a mining and iron-smelting area in Germany, developed the Neptunian theory. He suggested that all rocks, which were laid down as a great ocean covering the Earth, subsided starting with granites. Meanwhile a Scottish gentleman-farmer, James Hutton, put forward the Vulcan or Plutonian theory that rocks such as granite were formed by the flowing (intrusion) of molten magma into overlying rocks. Werner's theory was supported by Bible followers who saw Noah's flood as a defining moment in the Earth's history. Werner, however, did not accept the Bible stories. Hutton, on the other hand, was a staunch believer in the Biblical creation, although his theory was at odds with descriptions in Genesis. Hutton also suggested that the rocks on the surface of the Earth passed through a slow process of erosion, transport, sedimentation and uplift.

Charles Lyell developed Hutton's ideas further into the theory of uniformitarianism, which is that the processes of change that are happening today are the same ones that have happened throughout the history of the Earth, and although change is continually happening slowly, overall everything basically remains the same. Lyell saw no beginning to the history of the Earth, and presumed that the Earth went through periods when first one group of creatures were dominant and then others took over. Lyell's ideas, published in his *Principles of Geology* (a book which influenced Charles Darwin), were in opposition to the catastrophe theories of scientists such as Baron Georges Cuvier and Jean Louis Agassiz. The catastrophists said that the whole of the Earth's surface periodically underwent a radical change, during which extinctions of whole classes of living things took place. Noah's flood was just one of these great events.

On his travels, Darwin saw evidence of local catastrophes – earthquakes, volcanoes, and floods – but also saw the results of millennia of slow changes. This confirmed for him Lyell's description of what we now refer to as the rock cycle, including the formation of metamorphic rocks.

The age of the Earth

By the early nineteenth century, most scientists realised that Archbishop Ussher's calculation did not give a long enough timescale for the changes observed on the surface of the Earth. Gradually geologists' estimates of the age of the surface grew to over a hundred million years – for many people a staggeringly long period of time. But there was a problem. Scientists reasoned that if the Bible stories were not true, the Earth must have formed as a molten ball of rock. William Thomson (Lord Kelvin) was one of the leading authorities on energy, temperature and cooling. He calculated that the Earth could not have taken more than about 20 million years to cool from a molten state to the temperatures experienced now. This was not long enough for the geologists and caused a major problem in the 1890s.

When radioactivity was discovered, Ernest Rutherford realised that radioactive elements in the Earth's core kept the Earth hot, so the Earth would have taken much longer to cool to its present temperature. The geologists could have their hundreds of millions of years. It was Arthur Holmes who applied the new knowledge of radioactive decay to dating rocks. He soon found rocks that gave ages of over 300 million years, and in 1913 he was able to date the Earth as being 1600 million years old. Later in his life he increased his estimate to around 4 billion years.

Shrinking planet or moving continents?

At the turn of the twentieth century, one of the favoured explanations for the formation of mountain ranges was that the Earth had shrunk causing the surface to crack and crumple. For an astronomer-turned-meteorologist called Alfred Wegener, another idea seemed feasible. In talks, papers and books from 1910 onwards Wegener put forward his theory of continental drift. He thought that the landmasses moved through the underlying, denser rocks that formed the ocean floor. Wegener reckoned that, 200 million years ago, there had been just one continent, which he called Pangaea. Pangaea had split up and the continents had moved slowly to their present positions. As they moved, the edges of the continents crumpled up, forming mountain ranges such as the Rockies and Andes in the Americas.

Wegener's theory was rejected by most geologists. Despite the apparent match in the shapes of some of the continents, and the discovery of similar rocks and fossils on adjacent continents, there was no evidence that the landmasses moved. Wegener's explanation that continental drift was caused by gravity and the influence of the Moon, were easily dismissed as these forces were too feeble to overcome the massive frictional forces between the landmasses and the underlying rocks. Geologists preferred the idea of land bridges to account for the similarity of the fossils on different continents, despite the fact that no trace of any land bridge between continents had been found. Wegener died in 1930 on an expedition to the Greenland ice-cap, seeking more evidence to support his theory.

From continental drift to plate tectonics

From the 1920s to the 1960s, most geologists continued to dismiss the idea that the continents moved, but Wegener's idea would not go away. Soon after Wegener's death, Arthur Holmes suggested that convection currents in the mantle under the Earth's crust could provide sufficient force to move the landmasses.

In the 1930s, the science of oceanography began to provide answers to questions but also to pose more questions. The Second World War gave an enormous boost to the study of the sea-bed. Increasing use of submarines in the 1940s and 1950s demanded detailed maps of the ocean floor. Ultrasonic range finders were developed to probe the sea floor, and deep-sea submersibles were developed to bring samples from the depths. Many scientists, particularly in the USA, contributed to the expansion of knowledge about the oceans, although we refer to just a few of them on this CD. Seismic surveys had by this time revealed the layered structure of the Earth.

A ridge in the middle of the Atlantic Ocean had been discovered by the entrepreneurs who laid the first transatlantic telegraph cable in the mid-nineteenth century. Maurice Ewing's extensive surveys revealed the full extent of the ridge, and of ridges in the other oceans. He found that they had a central rift. Ewing also discovered that sediment generally increased in depth away from the ridge, whereas it had been expected to be fairly even across the ocean floor.

Harry Hess, an early supporter of continental drift, discovered many young formations on the ocean floor and suggested that Ewing's discoveries showed that the sea floor was spreading from the mid-ocean rifts. He also suggested that deep ocean trenches were places where the ocean floor was being forced down into the Earth's mantle, areas that were called subduction zones.

The final key piece of evidence supporting Hess' idea came from a prediction made by the British geologist, Frederick Vine, and his supervisor at Princeton University, Drummond Matthews. It had been known for some decades that the Earth's magnetic poles 'flipped' over from time to time. Rocks formed from molten magma contain magnetic minerals and as the magma cools they become magnetised by the Earth's magnetic field. Vine suggested that if rocks were being continuously formed at the mid-ocean ridges then they should carry a record of the shifts in the Earth's magnetic poles. American surveyors discovered the evidence at the same time as Vine made his prediction – a symmetrical pattern of the magnetic field in the rocks on either side of one of the oceanic ridges.

John Tuzo Wilson developed the idea of moving plates to explain all these discoveries. The idea became called 'the theory of plate tectonics'. Unlike Wegener's idea, the theory of plate tectonics saw the whole surface of the Earth as being broken up into several slow-moving plates that variously move apart, collide, or slide past each other.

Environmental science

Environmental science is a relatively recent amalgamation of relevant bits of the sciences that relate to the environment, but scientists have been concerned about the state of the land, sea and the atmosphere for a long time. In this CD we have concentrated on some of the problems generated by atmospheric pollution.

14

The greenhouse effect

Discoveries of 'invisible' rays during the nineteenth century, and the development of spectroscopic techniques, led a number of scientists to wonder what effect the atmosphere had on radiation. John Tyndall, at the Royal Institution in London, developed the first instrument to measure the absorption of infra-red light by various gases. He found that, of the gases in the air, carbon dioxide and water were by far the best absorbers. The Swedish chemist, Svante Arrhenius, considered what happened to the infra-red radiation emitted by the Earth and did a huge number of calculations. He suggested that the water and carbon dioxide in the air acted like a greenhouse, trapping some of the radiation and so warming the air and the surface of the Earth. This was important because, without this greenhouse effect, the Earth would be frozen and life as we know it would not be possible. Arrhenius noted that increased industrial activity was adding carbon dioxide to the air from the combustion of fossil fuels, and calculated that this would have an increased warming effect. He wasn't too worried, however, as he thought the warming would be beneficial.

During the 1920s there was some concern about the possibility of global warming and Guy Callendar added more data to Arrhenius'. However, from the 1930s to the 1950s global temperatures fell and concerns shifted to the possibility of a new ice age that would threaten human civilisation.

One problem was that there was not enough accurate data about the changes that might be occurring in the atmosphere. In the early 1950s, Charles Keeling took up the challenge to invent an instrument to measure the amount of carbon dioxide in the atmosphere accurately and at frequent intervals. His instrument was precise enough to show the diurnal changes in carbon dioxide levels as well as annual fluctuations. He set up one of his instruments on the Mauna Loa volcano in Hawaii in 1957. It has measured the inexorable rise of carbon dioxide in the atmosphere ever since, recording a 25% increase in the last century. Keeling's data was enough to convince his boss, Roger Revelle, that the enhanced greenhouse effect was real and that global warming was an inevitable and unwelcome consequence.

The difficulties in modelling changes in the climate across the Earth, and uncertainty about the fate of all the carbon dioxide released by burning fossil fuels, has allowed some scientists to dispute the actuality and the effects of global warming. At the start of the twenty-first century a consensus has been reached that the enhanced greenhouse effect is a serious environmental problem.

The ozone hole

The story of the stratospheric ozone crisis reveals that, while science can quickly solve one problem, it often fails to see the full consequences of the solution. It also shows that governments can act together in a crisis and holds out the hope that other environmental problems can be tackled.

The role of ozone in the stratosphere and the processes that produce it were discovered in the 1930s by Sidney Chapman, amongst others. Chemical reactions in the upper atmosphere absorb nearly all ultraviolet light, thus preventing it from reaching the Earth's surface where it could damage living cells. It was the formation of the ozone layer that allowed life to emerge from the seas onto the land, as water was no longer needed to protect cells from ultraviolet radiation.

At the same time that Chapman did his work Thomas Midgley made the second of his contributions to modern living by inventing CFCs (chlorofluorocarbons) for use in refrigerators. (He had earlier developed tetra-ethyl lead as a petrol additive to enhance engine performance in petrol-driven vehicles). By the 1960s and 1970s Midgley's compounds were also in use in aerosols, expanded plastics, fire extinguishers and as industrial solvents. They were ideal chemicals, non-flammable, non-corrosive, non-toxic, and available in many varieties.

James Lovelock realised that the properties of CFCs also meant that they would remain in the atmosphere for decades once they were released. He found measurable and increasing amounts of CFCs in the air, even in the Antarctic. Later in the 1970s Sherwood Rowland and Mario Molina became interested in the fate of CFCs. They were horrified to discover that when the CFCs reached the stratosphere, as they were bound to do, they would be split by the ultraviolet rays and start destroying the ozone that protected the surface of the Earth. At first their warnings went largely unheeded, although some uses of CFCs were restricted.

Meanwhile, Joe Farman had been taking measurements of the Antarctic atmosphere for years. In 1984 he realised that his data showed that the ozone was disappearing during the Antarctic spring. Strangely, NASA scientists who had data from polar satellites had not noticed the destruction of the ozone. When Farman's results were published NASA looked again at their records. It turned out that computers had been programmed to ignore anomalous results. The massive drop in ozone concentration was taken to be an instrument error and ignored. In fact, NASA had data recording the progressive growth of the ozone hole.

The consequences for life on Earth were obvious, and for once governments moved quickly to discuss the problem. By 1990 it was agreed to phase out the production and use of all CFCs. The problem is that many tonnes still remain in use in refrigerators and air conditioners and it will take a century for the CFCs already in the atmosphere to be removed by natural processes. It will be many decades before the ozone layer fully recovers.

E The characters

This section provides a brief summary of each character included in *Earth and the Environment*. They are presented here in the same order as they are presented in the text on the CD. In some cases this section provides additional information about events that occurred after the date that each character 'narrates' their life story in the CD text.

Abraham Gottlob Werner (1749–1817)

German mineralogist and geologist. Werner's family lived in Wehrau, now part of Poland, and were involved in mining and iron smelting. Werner studied at Freiberg Mining Academy and then at the University of Leipzig before returning to Freiberg to teach at the Academy.
He developed the Neptunian theory of the formation of rocks from the ocean and a classification scheme for rocks.

James Hutton (1726–1797)

British geologist. Hutton was born in Edinburgh, and studied law and medicine in Edinburgh, Paris and Leiden.
He inherited a farm in Berwick, which he spent nearly two decades improving, and developed an interest in soils and rocks. He returned to Edinburgh in 1788 as a gentleman of independent means.
Hutton pursued science, especially geology, and proposed his Vulcan or Plutonian theory for the formation of igneous rocks. It was published in 1788.
He also noted the erosive power of water and the long period of time required for geological processes.

Charles Lyell (1797–1875)

British geologist. Lyell was born in Scotland, the son of a well-known botanist, and attended Oxford University where he learned about the geological ideas of the time. He travelled widely on the continent and, although he studied law, he never practised. His *Principles of Geology* was published in the early 1830s.
He subsequently became professor of geology at King's College, London, but gave up the post to continue his travels.
He developed Hutton's theory into uniformitarianism, describing the slow cyclical processes that occurred to the Earth's rocks. He was knighted in 1848 and became a baron in 1864. Although his work influenced Darwin, and they became friends, he did not accept the principle of evolution until the late 1860s and even then denied that it applied to humans.

Jean Louis Agassiz (1807–1873)

Swiss–American biologist. Agassiz was born in Switzerland and studied at various universities before becoming a follower of Baron Georges Cuvier in Paris. He became an authority on fossil fishes, but his most notable work was the discovery of the ice ages and the geological effects of glaciers. He moved to the USA in 1846. Always a supporter of the catastrophist theory, he rejected Darwin's theory of evolution. He also considered there to be several species of humans, which gave support to those who wished to continue enslaving the coloured races.

William Thomson (Lord Kelvin) (1824–1907)

British physicist. Thomson was born in Belfast, but moved to Glasgow at an early age when his father took a post at the university. He was a bright child, and attended the university from the age of ten, before studying in Cambridge.
He returned to Glasgow and remained at the university for the rest of his life.
He did groundbreaking work in electromagnetism and thermodynamics, but also made a fortune from inventing scientific instruments and from advising on the transatlantic telegraph cable.
He applied his understanding of thermodynamics to work out the time taken for the Earth to cool from a molten ball of rock. He arrived at a value

much lower than that required by most geologists. This was because the heating effect of radioactive decay within the Earth was not known about at the time. He was made Baron Kelvin of Largs in 1892, in recognition of his contributions to science.

Alfred Wegener (1880–1930)
German meteorologist and geologist. Wegener was born in Berlin and studied astronomy. In 1906 he went to Greenland for the first time to carry out meteorological research, and on his return he became a lecturer at the university in Marburg. He fought in the First World War, was wounded twice, and he developed his theory of continental drift while recovering from these wounds. The outcry over his theory made it difficult for him to return to academic life but he continued with his expeditions to Greenland. He died there while trying to return from an outpost on the ice-cap to the main base on the coast.

Arthur Holmes (1890–1965)
British geologist. Holmes was born into a farming family in north-east England. He went to Imperial College in London where he studied geology, but he also became interested in radioactivity. After an expedition to Mozambique he developed radioactive techniques for dating rocks. Having married, he spent two years in the 1920s in Burma prospecting unsuccessfully for oil. After his return he was appointed professor of the new geology department at Durham University, where he proposed that convection currents could provide the driving force to move the continents. He achieved a high eminence in geology and his book on the *Principles of Physical Geology* was a popular textbook for many years.

William Maurice Ewing (1906–1974)
American oceanographer. Ewing was born in Texas, where he studied before moving to New York in 1944 to run the Lamont Geological Observatory. He used seismic

data to calculate the depth of the Earth's crust and advised the Navy during the Second World War. After the war, he and others embarked on many survey trips. They discovered the extent of the mid-ocean ridges and the depth of sediment on the ocean bed, both of which provided evidence for sea-floor spreading.

Harry Hammond Hess (1906–1969)
American geologist. Hess was born in New York and studied at Yale. After fieldwork in what is now Zambia, he took up a post at Princeton University. He became an officer in the Navy to get on board submarines surveying the sea-bed, and served at sea throughout the Second World War. Later, oceanographic surveys showed that much of the ocean floor was made of young rocks and he developed the theory of sea-floor spreading and subduction zones to explain the observations. He published his *History of Ocean Basins* in 1962.

Frederick Vine (1939–1988)
British geologist. Vine studied at Cambridge University. While he was a research student under Drummond Matthews, he predicted that, if Hess' theory of sea-floor spreading was correct, rocks on either side of mid-ocean ridges would show bands of alternating magnetic fields. This would happen because rocks were slowly and steadily being formed at the mid-ocean ridges and, on cooling, would record the orientation of the Earth's magnetic field which alternates every few million years. Data obtained in 1962 confirmed the hypothesis and Vine showed that the symmetrical magnetic banding supported Hess' theory of sea-floor spreading. Vine was at Princeton from 1965 to 1970, and then returned to England to the University of East Anglia where he became professor of environmental science.

John Tuzo Wilson (1908–1993)
Canadian geophysicist. Wilson was born in Canada where both his parents were expert and well-known mountain climbers. He was educated in Toronto

and Princeton and worked for the Canadian Geological Survey. After serving in the Army during the Second World War he became professor of geophysics at Toronto University. He provided evidence to support the theory of continental drift and introduced the new term 'plate' to describe the structure of the Earth's crust. He introduced the idea of the transform fault that occurs when one plate slides past another.

John Tyndall (1820–1893)

British physicist. Tyndall was born in Ireland and after leaving school he worked for the Irish Ordnance Survey. He moved to Manchester to work for a railway company, but always wanted to further his education. He taught for a while at a school in Hampshire, then studied in Marburg, Germany. On his return to England he obtained a post at the Royal Institution and rose to succeed Faraday as its director in 1867. He had many scientific interests but his most noteworthy work was on radiant heat. He developed an instrument for measuring the transmission of infra-red radiation through gases. Tyndall did much to maintain the Royal Institution's role in popularising science and he helped to found the journal *Nature*. Having married late in life his young wife accidentally killed him by confusing the dose of a sleeping drug that he took.

Svante Arrhenius (1859–1927)

Swedish physical chemist. Arrhenius was born near Uppsala in Sweden and attended the local university. Finding the standard poor, he transferred to Stockholm where he did research on electrical conduction in solutions. His research paper on ionic dissociation did not meet with his examiners' approval and he was given the lowest possible pass grade. However other eminent scientists saw the value of his work and in 1895 Arrhenius became a professor at Stockholm Technical University. He was awarded the Nobel Prize in 1903. He had many scientific interests, amongst which

was what he called the glasshouse effect (and we call this the greenhouse effect).

Guy Callendar (1897–1964)

British engineer. Callendar was born in Canada, but the following year his family returned to England. His father was a highly respected engineer who carried out important research on the properties of high temperature steam, as used in turbines. After school and college Callendar joined his father at Imperial College. His father died in 1930. He developed an interest in meteorology and extended Arrhenius' work on the greenhouse effect.

Charles Keeling (born 1928)

American meteorologist. Keeling was born in Scranton, Pennsylvania, and attended the University of Illinois and Northwestern University before moving to Caltech in Pasedena, California, in 1953. He soon began to build an instrument to measure the concentration of carbon dioxide in the atmosphere to an accuracy of one part per million. In 1956 he moved to Scripps Institute of Oceanography where the director, Roger Revelle, encouraged his work. In 1958 he set up a new carbon dioxide recorder on Mauna Loa in Hawaii and has maintained a constant record of the carbon dioxide concentration ever since.

Thomas Midgley (1889–1944)

American chemist. Midgley was born in Ohio, USA, where his father was an inventor and pioneer of motor cars. After studying engineering in New York he worked for the National Cash Register Company and then for his father's business, which went bankrupt in 1916. He then joined Charles Kettering doing contract research for the motor industry. In the 1920s, he developed lead additives to improve the octane rating of petrol. In 1928 the Frigidaire Company asked him to find a more suitable refrigerant and he developed CFCs.

19

Sidney Chapman (1888–1970)

British mathematician and geophysicist. Chapman was born in Manchester to strict non-conformist parents. It was intended that he should enter the family textile business, but friends helped him achieve scholarships to Manchester and Cambridge Universities where he studied mathematics. He used his skills to tackle the gas laws and then the Earth's magnetic field. He was a pacifist in the First World War but this did not stop him from working at the Greenwich Observatory. After the war he became professor at Manchester University and later Imperial College, becoming an authority on geomagnetism and in particular the magnetosphere. In the Second World War he assisted the Army and then moved to Oxford University. Not prepared to retire at the normal age of 65, he took on visiting professorships in Alaska and Colorado, and remained active until his death.

James Lovelock (born 1919)

British scientist. Lovelock was born in Hertfordshire and enjoyed roaming the countryside during his childhood.
He attended evening classes at Birkbeck College in London before gaining a place at Manchester University.
He graduated during the Second World War and then did war research at the National Institute for Medical Research. There he pioneered the use of microwaves for heating and developed an instrument for detecting low concentrations of molecules in the atmosphere. In 1961 he went to the USA to work for NASA on planetary space probes, but in 1964 he decided to become an independent researcher.
He used his own instrument in 1971 to detect CFCs in the Antarctic air.
His most well known work is the theory of Gaia, that the life on Earth is a single self-regulating organism.

Frank Sherwood Rowland (born 1927)

American chemist. Rowland was born in Ohio, USA, where his parents were lecturers. He was called up during the Second World War but did not see active service, and then went to university in Ohio and Chicago. He completed his PhD in 1952, then worked in Princeton and in Kansas before moving to the University of California in 1964.
In 1973, Mario Molina, one of his students, brought him some interesting figures on CFCs and together they discovered the effect of CFCs on ozone in the atmosphere. Rowland and Molina were awarded the Nobel Prize, along with Paul Crutzen, in 1995.

Joe Farman (born 1935)

British geophysicist. Farman has worked for the British Antarctic Survey since the late 1950s. In the early 1980s his measurements in the Antarctic showed that there was a severe reduction in the concentration of ozone in the atmosphere during the spring. His paper on the subject persuaded NASA to re-examine its own data and drew attention to the ozone crisis caused by CFCs.

Contemporary fictional characters

Aiko Enoki
A seismologist studying earthquakes in Japan.

Neil Stone
A British geologist working for a mining and quarrying company.

Josh Denton
An American creationist.

Nande Shabalala
A South African who attended the Earth Summit of world governments in Johannesburg in 2002.

Ray Marlowe
A scientific advisor to the president of the USA.

A TV presenter and four teenage characters are also provided but have no associated text.

F Matching charts

Matching chart for English National Curriculum and *Earth and the Environment*

Key Stage 3 Sc1 Scientific enquiry

		Statement	Activity
1	a	About the interplay between empirical questions, evidence and scientific explanations using historical and contemporary examples (for example, Lavoisier's work on burning, the possible causes of global warming).	1.1, 1.2, 2.1, 2.2, 3.1, 3.2, 4.1, 4.2, 5.1, 5.2, 6.1, 6.2
	b	That it is important to test explanations by using them to make predictions and by seeing if evidence matches the predictions.	4.1, 4.2, 5.1, 5.2, 6.1 6.2
	c	About the ways in which scientists work today and how they worked in the past, including the roles of experimentation, evidence and creative thought in the development of scientific ideas.	1.1, 1.2, 2.1, 2.2, 3.1, 3.2, 4.1, 4.2, 5.1, 5.2, 6.1, 6.2

Key Stage 4 Sc1 Scientific enquiry

		Statement	Activity
1	a	How scientific ideas are presented, evaluated and disseminated (for example, by publication, review by other scientists).	3.1, 3.2, 5.1, 5.2
	b	How scientific controversies can arise from different ways of interpreting empirical evidence (for example, Darwin's theory of evolution).	1.1, 1.2, 2.1, 2.2, 3.1, 3.2, 4.1, 4.2, 5.1, 5.2
	c	Ways in which scientific work may be affected by the contexts in which it takes place (for example, social, historical, moral and spiritual), and how these contexts may affect whether or not ideas are accepted.	2.1, 2.2, 3.1, 3.2, 6.1 6.2
	d	To consider the power and limitations of science in addressing industrial, social and environmental questions, including the kinds of questions science can and cannot answer, uncertainties in scientific knowledge, and the ethical issues involved.	5.1, 5.2, 6.1, 6.2

Matching chart for Welsh National Curriculum and *Earth and the Environment*

Key Stage 3 Sc1 Scientific enquiry

		Statement	Activity
1		**The Nature of Science**	
	2	To consider different sources of information, including that obtained from their own work and information from secondary sources.	1.1, 1.2, 2.1, 2.2, 3.1, 3.2, 4.1, 4.2, 5.1, 5.2, 6.1, 6.2
	3	How creative thought as well as information may be required in arriving at scientific explanations.	1.1, 1.2, 2.1, 2.2, 3.1, 3.2, 4.1, 5.1, 5.2
	4	About the work of scientists and the role of experimental data, creative thought and values in their work and in developing scientific ideas.	1.1, 1.2, 2.1, 2.2, 3.1, 3.2, 4.1, 4.2, 5.1, 5.2, 6.1, 6.2
2		**Communication in Science**	
	4	To search systematically for, process and analyse information for a specific purpose, using ICT to do so on some occasions.	1.1, 1.2, 2.1, 2.2, 3.1, 3.2, 4.1, 4.2, 5.1, 5.2, 6.1, 6.2

Key Stage 4 Sc1 Scientific enquiry

		Statement	Activity
1		**The Nature of Science**	
	2	To use and consider a variety sources of information, both that obtained from their own work and secondary sources, including ICT.	1.1, 1.2, 2.1, 2.2, 3.1, 3.2, 4.1, 4.2, 5.1, 5.2, 6.1, 6.2
	4	To recognise that scientific controversies arise from different interpretations and emphases placed on information.	1.1, 1.2, 2.1, 2.2, 3.1, 3.2
	5	To consider the ways in which scientific ideas are affected by social, political and historical contexts in which they develop, and how these contexts may affect whether or not the ideas are accepted.	1.1, 1.2, 2.1, 2.2, 3.1, 3.2, 4.1, 4.2, 5.1, 5.2

Earth and the Environment and English National Curriculum

Sc3 Materials and their properties

Statement covered	Key Stage 3	Key Stage 4
	2d, 2e, 2f, 2i	2p, 2q, 2r

Sc4 Physical processes

Statement covered	Key Stage 3	Key Stage 4
	1d	3f, 3m, 3n, 6f

Earth and the Environment and Welsh National Curriculum

Sc3 Materials and their properties

Statement covered	Key Stage 3	Key Stage 4
	2.6, 2.7, 2.12	2.24, 2.25

Sc4 Physical processes

Statement covered	Key Stage 3	Key Stage 4
	–	3.12

Matching chart for 5-14 Environmental Studies: Science and *Earth and the Environment*

	Statement	Activity
Materials from Earth	**Level D**	
	Describe the internal structure of the Earth.	2.2
	Describe the processes that led to the formation of the three main types of rock.	1.1, 1.2
Changing materials	**Level D**	
	Describe the effect of burning fossil fuels.	5.1, 5.2

Northern Ireland Programme of study for KS3 and KS4 and *Earth and the Environment*

Earth and the Environment can be used to teach the following parts of the Northern Ireland Programme of study for KS3:
PHYSICAL PROCESSES *Energy – j*
Earth and the Environment can be used to teach the following parts of the Northern Ireland Programme of study for KS4:
MATERIALS AND THEIR USES *Properties and uses – f*

1 Making rocks

Learning objectives

Students have the opportunity to learn:
- how different types of rock are formed
- how rocks are weathered and eroded
- about different theories that were put forward in the past to explain rock formation
- about different theories about how rocks are changed with time.

Learning outcomes

Students:
- answer questions by extracting information from text provided (Activity 1.1, Activity 1.2)
- make a set of display posters explaining our current ideas of rock formation and the rock cycle (Activity 1.1)
- summarise our current ideas about how rocks are changed over time (Activity 1.2).

Activity levels

Activity	KS3	KS4
1.1	All	All
1.2	Most	Most

NC Statements

	Sc1	Sc3
KS3	1a, 1c	2d, 2e, 2f
KS4	1b	2r

Background information

It was in the eighteenth century that the science of geology developed and attracted the attention of many European gentlemen. Werner and Hutton were amongst those who observed the rocks around where they lived or on their travels and speculated about their formation. Werner and Hutton proposed two very different theories which attracted supporters. From the 1820s Charles Lyell influenced many scientists and his book, *The Principles of Geology* outlined many of the processes that we understand today.

Prior knowledge

Activity 1.1 refers to igneous, sedimentary and metamorphic rocks, and it will be helpful if students have already met these terms and examined rock specimens. It will also be useful if they have studied the rock cycle, as these activities are best used as a reinforcement of existing knowledge about weathering, erosion and rock formation, in addition to looking at the development of scientific ideas.

Activity 1.1 Explaining the rock cycle

This activity looks at our modern ideas about rock formation, weathering and erosion, as told by the scientists who first put forward these ideas. Part A of the activity provides questions to allow students to extract basic information from the text. Part C asks students to make a set of display posters explaining the rock cycle, and a list of suggested headings is provided in the Word document 'Activity 1.1C'.

Activity 1.2 Different theories

Frames 1 to 17 of this activity look at two theories that were used to explain the formation of rocks – the Neptunian and Plutonist theories. The activity is in the form of an interview, and students are asked to answer the questions using the text. Activity 1.2C asks students to look at Frames 18 onwards, which deal with catastrophism and uniformitarianism. Students need to summarise the thoughts of each scientist.

Characters:	Werner, Hutton, Lyell, Stone, Simon, TV presenter.
Backgrounds:	TV studio, Hutton's Edinburgh, Lyells Volcano, Werner's quarry, modern quarry.
Props:	pictures of granite, limestone and slate, poster of rock cycle, posters showing Neptunian and Plutonian theories.

Lesson ideas

➧ Students may need access to textbooks for Part C of Activity 1.1 (making posters to summarise the rock cycle).

➧ As a starter activity pairs of students could be given a prepared 'domino'. One half of the domino bears the name of a rock and the other half bears the type of the rock. The students have to find two other dominoes, one to match each end of their domino, i.e. another named rock which matches the type of rock on the original domino, and a type of rock which matches the original rock. This gives the students three dominoes, with three names of rocks and three types of rock.

➧ An alternative starter is as follows: students in a class could be divided into teams of three. One team of three would play against another team of three. A chairperson would be needed for each pair of teams. The two teams would challenge each other to name the greatest number of a given type of rock. For example, the first team might say that they can name four types of igneous rock and the second may reply that they can name five. The chairperson would have the appropriate lists to check. The answers would have to be correct for the number the team said that they could give.

➧ Students may well have met the idea of the rock cycle before. It could be a useful lesson idea for them to design a revision sheet on the rock cycle. These revision sheets could be exchanged between students. They could be shown the format of revision guides and use some of these ideas. This has the advantage of generating lots of activities teachers could use and some interactive display work. A variation could be to do an A–Z of words associated with the topics, or to look for the weirdest word associated with the topic – tsunami, for example.

➧ Many of the processes involved in the rock cycle can be modelled by demonstrations. Descriptions of these can be found in standard texts. This could be arranged as a circus of demonstrations, or pairs of students could be allocated an experiment which they would demonstrate to the class, after appropriate safety checks. Students can often be quite inventive at modifying the basic method.

➧ Teachers and students could design a trail around the school or town to show different kinds of rocks and their uses. The uses of rocks often interest students more than the scientific approach and provide a good way to discuss the uses of rock in different ways such as sculpture and building.

➧ The rock cycle, as it is a sequence, lends itself to 'Just a minute' type exercises. As a plenary activity students could be asked to talk for one minute about the rock cycle. At the end of the minute the next student has to pick up the story. The teacher can introduce various levels of difficulty for example no hesitation or no repetition. Students generally listen very attentively to catch other students out on repetition.

➧ Students can be asked to invent and draw a machine, or a sequence of machines, which could perform the various phases of the rock cycle. This activity would work best if students were in pairs, or if bits of the rock cycle were allocated to named students.

Answers to homework questions

1 Their ideas were published in books. Werner was a lecturer, and so his students learned his theory. Students may suggest books or lectures, or even letters to friends.

2 a) Werner's observations were only in the area of Central Europe where he lived. Hutton's observations were made all over Europe.

b) Just once – all rocks were formed when the ocean that covered the Earth receded.

c) Many times – rocks were formed, but then weathered and eroded, and more rocks were formed from the sediments. This cycle could happen repeatedly.

d) Hutton's – he said that rocks could be folded, whereas Werner thought they were all laid down in roughly horizontal layers.

e) Hutton's. In Werner's theory, the granites were all formed first, so must always be older than the other types of rock. In Hutton's theory, molten rock could be forced into existing layers of rock, and would therefore be younger than these layers.

3 Hutton's theory could explain more of the features of rocks that could be seen in different parts of the world.

4 Any suitable key that works.

5 Granites have crystals of different colours, sandstones consist of grains of one mineral. Sandstones sometimes contain fossils, but granites never do.

6 Suitable rock cycle diagram, with sensible explanations of the terms used on the diagram.

7 Werner was a linguist as well as a geologist. He discovered eight new minerals during the course of his life as well as developing the Neptunian theory. Hutton retained his interest in farming all his life. He was also a Philosopher.

1 Making rocks

There have been many different ideas put forward to explain the formation of different kinds of rocks. Our modern ideas are based on the work of scientists who lived about 200 years ago.

1.1 Explaining the rock cycle

A Open storyboard 'Activity 1.1'. The frames show part of a TV documentary. There are some questions at the bottom of each frame. Use the text/audio symbol (the blue book) to find the answers to the questions. You can use the search box at the top right of the text to look for key words. Type your answers into the bottom window in your own words, or copy and paste from the text.

B Make your storyboard more interesting by adding frames with speech bubbles so that the characters can answer the questions themselves. You could add props or sound effects, or record your own audio track to make the characters speak for themselves. You can also add more human interest to the storyboard, by adding frames to show the interviewer finding out about the life stories of the characters.

C Use the information you have found out to write a set of display posters for a geology museum, explaining the rock cycle. To help you, we have provided some notes and a writing frame in Word, called 'Activity 1.1C', which you will find in your 'My Storyboards' folder. You can use images from Kar2ouche®, to illustrate your article, by copying them and pasting them into your word processing program.

1.2 Different theories

A Open storyboard 'Activity 1.2'. Frames 1 to 17 show an interview with scientists who had different theories about how rocks were formed. Click on the text/audio symbol (the blue book) to look at and listen to the text. You can use the search box at the top right of the text to look for key words. Add speech bubbles or audio to make the scientists answer the interviewer's questions.

B Continue Activity 1.2 from Frame 18 onwards. These frames show Sir Charles Lyell being interviewed about two different theories of how rocks are changed. Add speech bubbles or audio to make the characters answer the interviewer's questions.

1 Making rocks

Abraham Werner lived in Central Europe in the eighteenth century. He studied the rocks of the area and identified different types of rock. Some of the layers of rock contained fossils of fish and other sea creatures. Beneath the layers of sandstone, limestone and clays, Werner found granites.

I suggest that about one million years ago a vast ocean covered the Earth's surface. All the substances that form rocks were dissolved in the water. Gradually the substances began to crystallise and settle on the bottom of the ocean. The first rocks to be formed were the granites and basalts. Then the other rocks were deposited in turn, one layer above the other.

James Hutton lived at approximately the same time as Werner. He travelled all over Europe and looked at the structures of rocks in many places. Eventually he settled in Edinburgh, a city built on volcanic rocks. The castle high above the city was built on a volcanic outcrop that thrust through the surrounding rocks.

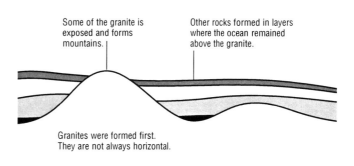

Some of the granite is exposed and forms mountains.

Other rocks formed in layers where the ocean remained above the granite.

Granites were formed first. They are not always horizontal.

I suggest that there is heat under the surface of the Earth and that this heat keeps rock in a molten state below the land. In volcanoes this molten rock comes to the surface as lava. But often, when the molten rock pushes up the overlying rocks, it does not break out on to the surface and instead cools underground to form granite. The rocks on the surface can be folded and bent by movements of the Earth, and are slowly worn down by the forces of the weather. New rocks can be formed from the sediments made by weathering, and these rocks, in their turn, will be weathered and eroded.

1 Making rocks (cont.)

1 Both theories had their supporters. How do you think people in the eighteenth century learned about Hutton's and Werner's theories?

2 a) Werner and Hutton both based their theories on observations. Where did each man carry out his observations?

   b) How many times did Werner think that rocks had been formed? Explain your answer.

   c) How many times did Hutton think that rocks could be formed? Explain your answer.

   d) Whose theory could explain why layers of rock were not always horizontal? Explain your answer.

   e) Whose theory could explain why granites are sometimes younger than the layers of rock around them? Explain your answer.

3 Werner's theory was popular for many years, particularly with people who believed in the truth of the story of Noah and the Flood in the Bible. Why do you think most geologists eventually preferred Hutton's theory?

4 Design a key to identify some rocks using the following descriptions:

   Granite is a hard rock consisting of many crystals of various colours. It does not contain fossils and does not react with acids.

   Sandstone is a fairly soft rock consisting of grains of quartz that rub off quite easily. Sandstones sometimes contain fossils but do not react with acids.

   Limestone is a fairly soft rock consisting of grains which rub off quite easily. It sometimes contains fossils and fizzes in acid.

   Marble is a hard crystalline rock, which does not contain fossils and fizzes in acid.

5 Werner was able to identify different rocks by their appearance. How does a sample of granite differ from a piece of sandstone?

6 Charles Lyell and other geologists later developed Werner's and Hutton's theories into the rock cycle that we accept today. Draw a diagram of the rock cycle, using the following labels. Explain what each label means.

upthrust   weathering   transport   sedimentation   erosion
magma cooling   heat and pressure   igneous   sedimentary   metamorphic

 Use books or the Internet to find out more about:

7 a) The Biblical story of Noah and the Flood, or the Flood stories that occur in other religions, and the reasons why many Christians thought that this fitted with Werner's theory.
   OR
   b) The life stories of Werner and Hutton.

You can find some website addresses at **www.peopleinscience.co.uk**.

2 Collecting evidence

Learning objectives

Students have the opportunity to learn:
- how ideas about the age of the Earth have changed
- about the views of creationists on the age of the Earth
- how radioactivity can be used to provide evidence for the age of rocks
- how geologists investigate the structure of the Earth using seismic waves
- why the prediction of earthquakes and volcanic eruptions is difficult.

Learning outcomes

Students:
- answer questions by extracting information from text provided (Activity 2.1, Activity 2.2)
- write encyclopaedia entries on different ways of finding out about the Earth and its structure (Activity 2.2).

Activity levels

Activity	KS3	KS4
2.1	All	All
2.2	Some	Most

NC Statements

	Sc1	Sc4
KS3	1a, 1c	1d
KS4	1b, 1c	3m, 3n, 6f

Background information

For most of history people have believed that the Earth was no older than the oldest known human civilisations. However, during the nineteenth century geological theories began to demand a much longer time-scale. Even the calculations carried out by Lord Kelvin, which assumed that the Earth had been cooling since its formation, could not provide the hundreds of millions of years that were required. The discovery of radioactivity changed all that and also provided a means for the measurement of the age of rocks.

After the Second World War scientists, encouraged by military interests, gained new tools for probing beneath the Earth's surface which lead to a revolution in our understanding of the structure of the Earth. Seismic waves help to tell geologists a lot about the structure of the Earth because they are refracted at different speeds by layers of the Earth.

Prior knowledge

Students working on Activity 2.2 would benefit from having a basic understanding of radioactivity and waves.

Activity 2.1 How old is the Earth?

This activity traces changing ideas about the age of the Earth. Part A of the activity provides questions to allow students to extract information from the text. Part C asks students to extend the storyboard by explaining the viewpoint of creationists, who hold that the Earth is only about 6000 years old.

Activity 2.2 How do they know?

This activity looks at how geologists collect evidence of different kinds. Students are asked to write a series of encyclopaedia entries using a word processor package. The entries are on radioactive dating, seismic waves, earthquake and eruption prediction. The frames in the storyboard give a suggested structure for each entry. You may wish to ask pupils to attempt only one or two entries. The work on earthquake and eruption prediction should be suitable for most students.

Characters:	Werner, Hutton, Kelvin, Holmes, Vine, Stone, Enoki, Jane, Azir, Denton.
Backgrounds:	TV studio, Hutton's Edinburgh, Holme's Lab, Thompson's University, Lyells Volcano, Werner's quarry, earthquake zone, modern quarry
Props:	diagrams of seismic waves, seismometer.

Lesson ideas

➡ Students will find question 3 on the homework sheet easier if they have done the earthquake and eruption prediction part of Activity 2.2.

The following activities can be used for starter or plenary sessions when introducing the idea that earthquakes and volcanoes are difficult to predict.

➡ Students could be asked to design an addition to a weather forecast, which warns of an earthquake or volcanic eruption. How would they design the visuals? What words would they use?

➡ Schools in the UK have fire regulations. What would earthquake regulations/earthquake drill be for a school in Los Angeles?

➡ Students could be asked to suggest and then research how buildings are protected against earthquakes.

➡ Students could be asked to investigate why diseases spread so quickly after earthquakes or volcanic activity. What sort of diseases are a problem?

➡ Students could work out a strategy for organising relief after earthquakes and volcano eruptions.

Answers to homework questions

1

Who made the estimate	Age of the Earth	Method used
Archbishop Ussher,1650	6000 years	adding up ages of people in the Bible
Abraham Werner, 1790s	1 million years	calculations of time taken for crystals to form from solution
Charles Lyell, 1830s	eternal	idea that there is unending cycle of changes in rocks
Lord Kelvin, 1880s	20 million years	calculations of time taken for molten rock to cool
Arthur Holmes, 1913	1600 million years	radioactive dating
modern estimates	4.6 billion years	radioactive dating

2 a) Radioactive dating of rocks.

b) Evolution takes a long time to happen, and if the Earth was not its present age, evolution would not have had time to produce the variety of living things that we see around us today.

c) They believe that what is written in the Bible is the truth.

3 a) By measuring the shape of the Earth, or by measuring the gases given off by volcanoes.

b) They do not know enough about what is happening inside the Earth.

c) So they can evacuate people and save lives.

d) Many people will not believe them the next time they predict an earthquake, and so might not follow safety warnings.

e) Students' answers might include fear for their property being destroyed or looted, annoyance at disruption to their lives, particularly if the eruption does not happen.

4 Earthquakes and volcanoes are usually centred on the edges of the tectonic plates. Students can find many eyewitness accounts on the Internet or in books.

2 Collecting evidence

2.1 How old is the Earth?

Museums often have exhibitions explaining science. Sometimes these exhibitions have films of actors pretending to be scientists explaining their ideas. You are going to make an exhibit that explains how and why ideas about the age of the Earth have changed.

A Open storyboard 'Activity 2.1'. The frames show different scientists who had ideas about the age of the Earth. At the bottom of each frame there are some questions.
Use the text/audio symbol (the blue book) to find the answers to the questions. You can use the search box at the top right of the text to look for key words. Type your answers into the bottom window in your own words, or copy and paste from the text.

B Make your storyboard more interesting by adding speech bubbles so that the characters can answer the questions themselves. You can also add props or sound effects, or record your own audio track to make the characters speak.

C Creationists believe that everything that is written in the Bible is true, and so they believe that the Earth was formed about 6000 years ago. Add some more frames to the storyboard to explain the views of the creationists, and why they think today's geologists are wrong. You will need to look at the text for Josh Denton.

2.2 How do they know?

A Open storyboard 'Activity 2.2'. The activity asks you to write a series of encyclopaedia entries explaining how geologists gather evidence for their theories. You will need to write your entries in a Word document.
Click on the text/audio symbol (the blue book) to look at and listen to the text. You can use the search box at the top right of the text to look for key words.
Your teacher may tell you which entries to write.

B Create images in Kar2ouche®, to illustrate your entries. Paste them into your Word document.

2 Collecting evidence

1   Many different people have tried to estimate the age of the Earth. The table shows the estimates of the Earth's age, the people who made them and the methods they used – but they are all muddled up. Make a copy of the table, and write the information in the correct order. (*Hint*: Start by putting the people in order, and remember that (apart from Lyell) each time someone made a new estimate, the Earth got older!)

Who made the estimate	Age of the Earth	Method used
Charles Lyell, 1830s	6000 years	calculations of time taken for molten rock to cool
Archbishop Ussher, 1650	1 million years	radioactive dating
modern estimates	20 million years	adding up ages of people in the Bible
Abraham Werner, 1790s	1600 million years	calculations of time taken for crystals to form from solution
Arthur Holmes, 1913	4.6 billion years	idea that there is an unending cycle of changes in rocks
Lord Kelvin, 1880s	eternal	radioactive dating

2   Most people today accept the 'old Earth' theory that the Earth was formed from a ball of molten rock, about 4.6 billion years ago. Some people do still believe the 'young Earth' theory that says that the Earth was created in its present form a few thousand years ago.
   a) What evidence is there that supports the 'old Earth' theory?
   b) Why do supporters of the theory of evolution also need the 'old Earth' theory?
   c) Why do you think that some people still believe the 'young Earth' theory?

It is very difficult to predict when earthquakes or eruptions will happen. We can make very accurate measurements of the Earth's surface, and sometimes we can tell that an earthquake will happen soon. However, we do not understand enough about what is happening to let us predict an exact date or a time. We can also measure volcanoes, and sometimes the volcano changes shape just before an eruption, or the gases it gives off change, but we can never be sure exactly when the eruption will happen.

2 Collecting evidence (cont.)

3 a) How can scientists attempt to predict when earthquakes or eruptions will happen?

  b) Why can't they predict an exact time?

  c) Why do governments need to know when an eruption or earthquake will happen?

  d) What do you think might happen if scientists warn of an earthquake, and then the earthquake does not happen?

  e) Imagine that you live near a volcano. The government have told you that you have to leave your home because an eruption might happen soon. Write down what you might feel about being moved away from your home, and what you might be worrying about.

 Use books or the Internet to find out more about:

4 a) The places on the Earth where volcanoes or earthquakes are likely to happen.
     OR

  b) The eruptions of Mount St Helens in 1980, or Mount Pinatubo in 1991, and the effects that these eruptions had on the local people.

You can find some website addresses at **www.peopleinscience.co.uk**.

3 Wegener's big idea

Learning objectives

Students have the opportunity to learn:
- about Wegener's theory of continental drift
- why Wegener's theory was not accepted at the time
- about the role of evidence in the acceptance of new scientific ideas.

Learning outcomes

Students:
- answer questions by extracting information from text provided (Activity 3.1, Activity 3.2)
- summarise Wegener's theory (Activity 3.1)
- summarise the reasons why Wegener's theory was not accepted at the time (Activity 3.2).

Activity levels

Activity	KS3	KS4
3.1	All	All
3.2	Most	All

NC Statements

	Sc1	Sc4
KS3	1a, 1c	-
KS4	1a, 1b, 1c	3n

Background information

Wegener was not the first to notice the curious fit of the continents, nor the first to suggest that perhaps the landmasses moved. He was, however, the first to collect and publish evidence for the proposition. His work was published in English after the First World War.

Few geologists supported him at this time. This was partly because he was not a member of the geologists 'club', but mainly because he had no plausible explanation for a force capable of moving the continents.

Prior knowledge

Students need to know what fossils are, and it will also be helpful (for Activity 3.2) if they have learned about convection.

Activity 3.1 Wegener and his theory

This activity shows Wegener describing his theory of continental drift. Part A of the activity provides questions to allow students to extract information from the text. Part C asks students to add a frame summarising Wegener's evidence for his theory and the reasons why it was not accepted.

Activity 3.2 Wegener versus the world

This activity presents a TV debate about why new scientific theories are not always accepted, using Wegener's theory of continental drift as the focus. Part A of the activity provides questions to help students to extract the required information from the text. Part C asks students to add a frame summarising the reasons why theories are not always accepted at first.

Characters:	Wegener, Holmes, Enoki, Marcia.
Backgrounds:	TV studio, Wegener's base.
Props:	poster of Pangaea.

Lesson ideas

➡ As a starter, you could show pupils the usual map of moving continents. However, make the map using newspaper, so that the lines of print run across the continents to illustrate how rocks can be matched.

➡ As a plenary exercise students could be encouraged to complete a story which begins: 'Think about it! You would have been able to walk from New York to London without getting your feet wet. This was a long time ago …'

38

Answers to homework questions

1

Statement	For or Against?
The shapes of the continents fit together, suggesting that they were once all one super-continent.	For
Wegener was not a geologist and had no experience of rocks and fossils.	Against
Wegener had no idea of what force could move the landmasses over the underlying rocks.	Against
The same rocks are found across two continents, for example in Brazil and West Africa.	For
Fossils of the same animals and plants are found on two or more continents.	For
Evolution suggests that this would be impossible unless they shared habitats.	For
There was no evidence that the continents were moving. The speed suggested by Wegener's theory was too small to be measured by the instruments available in the early twentieth century.	Against
Fossils of tropical plants and animals are found in Antarctica and in other cooler continents, suggesting that they were once closer to the Equator.	For
Each continent has its own particular animals and plants, for example the kangaroos of Australia.	Against
The Earth is not old enough for one continent to have broken up into all the separate continents we have today.	Against

2 The apparent fit of the continents may be a coincidence (and is not really as good as it looks on a small map). Land bridges once existed that allowed animals to move from one continent to another. Similar processes may have produced similar rocks on two continents. The climate may have been warmer across the whole Earth a long time ago.

3 a) He said that mountain ranges were formed when one continent pushed into another.

b) The Earth had shrunk as it cooled, and the crust crumpled up.

4 Accept a yes or no answer, as long as it is backed up by a sensible reason.

5 Wegener was also a meteorologist and was particularly interested in Greenland. He made several expeditions to Greenland and finally died there.

3 Wegener's big idea

3.1 Wegener and his theory

A Open storyboard 'Activity 3.1'. The frames show Alfred Wegener, who had the idea that the continents can move about the surface of the Earth.
There are some questions at the bottom of each frame. Use the text/audio symbol (the blue book) to find the answers to the questions. You can use the search box at the top right of the text to look for key words. Type your answers into the bottom window in your own words, or copy and paste from the text.

B Make your storyboard more interesting by adding props or sound effects, or by recording your own audio track to make Wegener speak for himself. You can also add more human interest to the storyboard, by adding frames to show Wegener telling more of his life story.

C Add an extra frame at the end of the storyboard to summarise Wegener's evidence for continental drift, and the reasons why other geologists did not accept his ideas.

3.2 Wegener versus the world

A Open storyboard 'Activity 3.2'. The frames show a discussion about Wegener's theory of continental drift, and why it was not accepted by other geologists. There are some questions at the bottom of each frame. Use the text/ audio symbol (the blue book) to find the answers to the questions. You can use the search box at the top right of the text to look for key words. Type your answers into the bottom window in your own words, or copy and paste from the text.

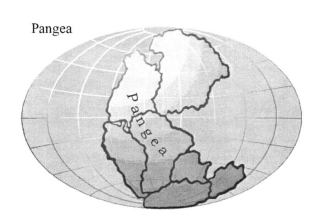

Pangea

B Add speech bubbles to make the characters explain for themselves, or record your own audio. Add extra frames if you need them. You can also make the frames look more interesting by adding props or different backgrounds.

C Add a frame at the end of the storyboard, showing Marcia summarising the reasons why Wegener's theory was not accepted by scientists at the time.

3 Wegener's big idea

Name _____ Date _____ Class _____

I noticed that the edges of the continents seemed to fit together. For example, South America fits neatly into West Africa. I was not the first person to see this, but I looked for other evidence to support my idea, such as similar rocks and fossils on different continents. I suggest that the landmasses, or continents, of the Earth 'float' on a layer of denser rocks similar to those found beneath the oceans. About 200 million years ago there was just one continent, which I call Pangaea. This super-continent broke up and the parts drifted apart to the positions they are in today, and mountains formed when one continent pushed into another. Unfortunately, I could not explain what made the continents move. I published my theory in Germany, and in 1922 it was published in English. It created a lot of debate but most geologists dismissed my ideas as nonsense.

When Wegener suggested his theory, most geologists thought that the continents had always been in the positions that they are in today. Most scientists agreed that the Earth was between 20 million and a few hundred million years old. They thought that it had cooled and shrunk over that time. The shrinking has caused the surface to crumple forming the mountain ranges. They suggested that the continents were once connected by 'land bridges' that allowed animals to roam from one continent to another. These land bridges had sunk into the sea, cutting off the creatures on one continent from those on the others. Very little was known about the rocks under the oceans.

3 Wegener's big idea (cont.)

1   Look at the following statements and decide whether they support Wegener's theory, or are arguments that other geologists might have used against the theory. Write 'For Wegener' or 'Against Wegener' in the last column of the table.

Statement	For or Against?
The shapes of the continents fit together, suggesting that they were once all one super-continent.	
Wegener was not a geologist and had no experience of rocks and fossils.	
Wegener had no idea of what force could move the landmasses over the underlying rocks.	
The same rocks are found across two continents, for example in Brazil and West Africa.	
Fossils of the same animals and plants are found on two or more continents.	
Evolution suggests that this would be impossible unless they shared habitats.	
There was no evidence that the continents were moving. The speed suggested by Wegener's theory was too small to be measured by the instruments available in the early-twentieth century.	
Fossils of tropical plants and animals are found in Antarctica and in other cooler continents, suggesting that they were once closer to the Equator.	
Each continent has its own particular animals and plants, for example the kangaroos of Australia.	
The Earth is not old enough for one continent to have broken up into all the separate continents we have today.	

2   Look at the statements that Wegener used in support of his theory. How might his opponents have explained the following things: same fossils on different continents, apparent fit of continents, similar rocks on different continents, finding fossils of tropical plants in Antarctica?

3   a) How did Wegener explain the formation of mountains?
    b) How did Wegener's opponents say that mountains had been formed?

4   Do you think that the scientific world was justified in rejecting Wegener's theory in the 1920s? Explain your answer.

 Use books or the Internet to find out more about:

5   a) How scientists think that the continents once fitted together when Pangaea existed.
       OR
    b) More about Wegener's life, his expeditions to Greenland and the other scientific subjects he was interested in.

You can find some website addresses at **www.peopleinscience.co.uk**.

4 Cracked Earth

Learning objectives
Students have the opportunity to learn:
➡ about the difference between the theories of continental drift and plate tectonics
➡ about the evidence that supports the theory of plate tectonics
➡ what happens at plate boundaries
➡ how the theory of plate tectonics can explain earthquakes, mountain formation and volcanoes.

Learning outcomes
Students:
➡ answer questions by extracting information from the text provided (Activity 4.1)
➡ summarise the evidence for the theory of plate tectonics, in the form of an encyclopaedia entry (Activity 4.1)
➡ extract information from the text and from external sources to describe tectonic plates and what happens at plate boundaries (Activity 4.2)
➡ assemble information into a logical sequence (Activity 4.2)
➡ summarise information to make a set of revision notes (Activity 4.2).

Activity levels

Activity	KS3	KS4
4.1	Some	All
4.2	Some	Most

NC Statements

	Sc1	Sc4
KS3	1a, 1b, 1c	–
KS4	1a, 1b	3n

Background information
Wegner's theory of continental drift was based on the idea that continents moved around on the surface of the Earth. Wegner thought that the continents moved on top of the rocks that form the sea-bed. In the 1950s and 1960s a huge amount of new data was collected that lead to the theory of plate tectonics. (The theory of plate tectonics suggests that the surface of the Earth is made of a series of plates which move on convection currents in the mantle.)

Many more people were involved in the story than are mentioned here, but the work of Vine, on the magnetic 'stripes' in rocks on either side of the mid-ocean ridge, is seen as the crucial step in the final acceptance of the theory by most scientists. The importance of military funding for the research (mapping the ocean floor for nuclear submarines) is an important ethical point.

Prior knowledge
It will be helpful if students know about Wegener's theory of continental drift, and why it was not accepted initially. It will also be helpful if they have briefly covered the theory of plate tectonics.

Activity 4.1 The evidence for plate tectonics
This activity looks at the evidence that supports the theory of plate tectonics. Part A of the activity provides questions to help students to extract the required information from the text. Part C asks students to write a summary of the evidence that could be used as an encyclopaedia entry.

Activity 4.2 Plate tectonics explains ...

This activity asks students to complete a teaching sequence explaining what happens at different types of plate boundaries. Part A provides a set of suggested headings and questions to be answered. Part C asks students to write a short summary of the key points that could be used for revision. Students will also need access to text books that cover plate tectonics.

Characters:	Wegener, Holmes, Ewing, Hess, Vine, Wilson, Enoki, Marcia.
Backgrounds:	TV studio, Ewing's ship, earthquake zone, Wegener's base.
Props:	posters of Pangaea, convection currents, oceanic and continental plates, continental plates and oceanic plates, mid-ocean ridge, magnetic stripes.

Lesson ideas

➡ Activity 4.2 asks students to provide a teaching sequence explaining what happens at plate boundaries. Students will need access to text books to complete this activity.

➡ If students have access to scissors and glue at home, they could cut out the statements in question 1 of the homework sheet and rearrange them to make the timeline. If they are to do this, the worksheet should not be copied onto both sides of a single piece of paper.

➡ As a plenary activity students could create a Mind Map™ with plate tectonics in the middle.

➡ Students could apply How, When, Where, Why, Who and What as the beginning of sentences which pose questions. Students could write these questions on cards which could be answered at intervals during the lessons.

➡ Students could be asked to research one piece of evidence for plate tectonics and present this to the class.

Answers to homework questions

1

- A ridge is found ... (observation).
- In the 1890s, Lord Kelvin ... (idea).
- During the 1900s, Ernest Rutherford ... (idea).
- In 1913, Arthur Holmes ... (observation).
- Alfred Wegener's theory ... (idea).
- In 1930, Arthur Holmes ... (idea).
- In the early 1950s, Maurice Ewing ... (observation).
- Maurice Ewing's surveys ... (observation).
- In 1962, Harry Hess ... (idea).
- When molten rock solidifies ... (prediction).
- In 1963, magnetic 'stripes' are found ... (observation).
- In the mid 1960s, John Tuzo Wilson ... (idea).

2 By publishing books and journals, or at conferences or lectures.

3 Submarines had to know the shape of the sea-bed to operate safely, and also to know about ocean currents, etc.

4 There was a lot more evidence to back up the idea of plate tectonics than Wegener had had for his theory.

5 Geologists use seismometers to scan the ocean floor. The seismometer picks up sound waves that are produced by the survey ship. The sound waves bounce off the ocean floor and the way that they are refracted tells us about the shape of the rocks and sediments. Mid-ocean ridges can be found in the Atlantic, Pacific and Indian oceans, as well as between the Antarctic and Australia.

4 Cracked Earth

4.1 The evidence for plate tectonics

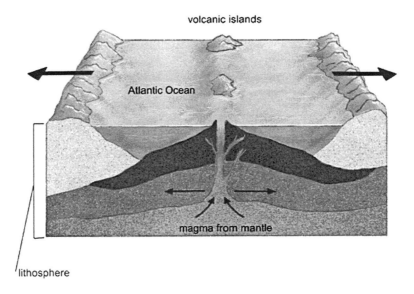

Mid ocean ridge

volcanic islands

Atlantic Ocean

magma from mantle

lithosphere

A Open storyboard 'Activity 4.1'. The frames show a documentary programme explaining the evidence for the theory of plate tectonics.
There are some questions at the bottom of each frame. Use the text/audio symbol (the blue book) to find the answers to the questions. You can use the search box at the top right of the text to look for key words. Type your answers into the bottom window in your own words, or copy and paste from the text.

B Make your storyboard more interesting by adding props or sound effects, or by recording your own audio track to make the characters speak for themselves. Add more frames if you need them.

C Write a short summary of the evidence for plate tectonics that could be used as an encyclopaedia entry.

4.2 Plate tectonics explains ...

The theory of plate tectonics can explain how mountain ranges form, why earthquakes happen, and why volcanoes erupt.

A Open storyboard 'Activity 4.2'. This shows the first frame of a sequence designed to teach secondary school students about plate tectonics. Frames 2 onward suggest some headings for the rest of the sequence.
Complete the teaching sequence using information from *People in Science*, and from text books. Use the images provided to illustrate your lesson.

B Make your lesson more interesting by recording an audio track, so students can listed instead of reading text from the screen.

C Use the information you have found out to write a short set of revision notes that summarise the key points.

4 Cracked Earth

1 Alfred Wegener's theory of continental drift may have been dismissed by geologists in the 1920s, but the idea would not go away. By the mid 1960s, enough evidence had been accumulated to convince most scientists.

   The boxes on the next page describe some of the ideas and evidence connected with the idea of moving continents. Cut out and stick the information in the correct order to make a timeline. Where you can, say if each statement describes an idea, a prediction, or an observation.

2 Many people are involved in the plate tectonics story. How do you think their discoveries and ideas were shared?

3 Why did the increasing use of submarines in the Second World War and afterwards help the science of oceanography (the study of the oceans and the ocean floor)?

4 Why do you think that in the 1960s people were prepared to accept the idea of plate tectonics, while in the 1920s Wegener's theory was rejected?

 Use books or the Internet to find out more about:

5 a) The instruments that are used for surveying the ocean floor.
      OR
   b) Where the mid-ocean ridges are on the Earth, and how many different tectonic plates there are.

You can find some website addresses at **www.peopleinscience.co.uk**.

A ridge is found in the middle of the Atlantic Ocean during the laying of the first transatlantic telegraph cable in the 1860s.	During the 1900s, Ernest Rutherford suggests that radioactivity could be heating the Earth, thus allowing the Earth to be hundreds of millions of years old.	Maurice Ewing's surveys in the 1950s also find that the ocean floor is much thinner than the continents, and that the amount of sediment on the ocean floor decreases the closer you get to the mid-ocean ridges.
In 1962, Harry Hess suggests that the ocean floor is spreading and that new rock is formed at the mid-ocean ridges. He also suggests that in deep ocean trenches, the dense ocean floor is being pushed under the lighter landmass in subduction zones.	When molten rock solidifies it becomes magnetised by the Earth's magnetic field. It was known that every few million years the Earth's north and south poles flip over. In the early 1960s, Frederick Vine suggests that a record of these flips should be recorded in the rocks on either side of the mid-ocean ridges.	In the mid 1960s, John Tuzo Wilson introduces the term 'plate tectonics' to explain the discoveries of Ewing, Hess, Vine and others. He suggests that the Earth's surface is broken up into plates which are moving. The plates are moving apart at mid-ocean ridges, colliding and forming mountain ranges or producing subduction zones, or sliding past each other.
In the early 1950s Maurice Ewing surveys the ocean floor. In 1956 he finds that the mid–Atlantic ridge stretches for the full length of the Atlantic Ocean and, in 1957, that it has a great rift at its centre.	In the 1890s, Lord Kelvin calculates that the Earth could not be more than 20 million years old if it has been cooling from a ball of molten rock.	In 1963 magnetic 'stripes' are found exactly as Vine predicts. The pattern is the same on either side of the ridge showing that the ocean floor is being pushed apart.
In 1913, Arthur Holmes uses radioactive dating of rocks to work out that the Earth must be at least 1600 million years old.	Alfred Wegener's theory of continental drift is published in English in 1922.	In 1930, Arthur Holmes suggests that heat from the centre of the Earth could produce convection currents in the rocks under the Earth's crust. The force of these convection currents could be enough to move the continents.

5 Global warming

Learning objectives
Students have the opportunity to learn:
- that the temperature of the Earth has changed in the past
- how the different gases in the atmosphere affect the temperature of the Earth
- that levels of carbon dioxide in the atmosphere are increasing due to the burning of fossil fuels
- that most scientists agree that increasing carbon dioxide levels will lead to global warming
- some possible consequences of global warming
- about some of the efforts being made to control carbon dioxide levels.

Learning outcomes
Students:
- extract information from the text and answer questions (Activity 5.1, Activity 5.2)
- summarise the evidence for global warming in the form of a magazine article (Activity 5.1)
- write about the efforts to control global warming, in the form of a newspaper article (Activity 5.2).

Activity levels

Activity	KS3	KS4
5.1	Most	All
5.2	Most	All

NC Statements

	Sc1	Sc3	BoS
KS3	1a, 1b, 1c	2i	1a, 1c
KS4	1b, 1c, 1d	2p, 2q	1a, 1c

Background information
Global warming has been newsworthy for some years now but concern about changing climate and its effects on civilisation has been expressed for over 100 years. Sometimes the worry has been that the world is heading for another ice age, at other times global warming has been seen as beneficial. Although the greenhouse effect was recognised in the nineteenth century, it was not until the 1950s that instruments existed that could monitor the changing carbon dioxide concentration in the atmosphere. Charles Keeling's graph of increasing carbon dioxide levels has become an icon of the climate change lobby.

The greenhouse effect is necessary to keep the Earth at its current relatively stable temperature. More carbon dioxide means that the normal greenhouse effect becomes enhanced, and this can lead to a significant rise in global temperatures, which may then lead to changes in climate and sea level.

Prior knowledge
Students should know that materials can absorb heat, and that warm materials radiate heat. They should also understand what fossil fuels are, and that burning fossil fuels produces carbon dioxide.

Activity 5.1 Warming or cooling?
This activity shows how ideas about the greenhouse effect and global warming have developed. Part A of the activity provides questions to help students to extract the required information from the text. Part C asks students to write a summary of the evidence that could be used as an article in a science magazine.

48

Activity 5.2 What should we do?

This activity shows various scientists and fictional characters being asked about global warming, its causes and effects. Part A of the activity provides questions to help students to extract the required information from the text. Part C asks students to write a newspaper article on the action that would need to be taken to reduce global warming.

Characters:	Agassiz, Tyndall, Arrhenius, Callendar, Keeling, Marlowe, Shabalala, Azir, Jane.
Backgrounds:	TV studio, Keeling's monitoring station, Tyndall's Lab, Arrhenius' study, Callendar's Lab, Mount Wilson.
Props:	Carbon dioxide graph, global warming placards.

Lesson ideas

➡ Students will need a sheet of graph paper to answer question 1 on the homework sheet.

➡ As a starter activity the teacher could give the class this statement: 'Global warming is beneficial'. Students could then see if they could both support and then oppose the statement.

➡ Students could be asked to research cars which run on hydrogen fuel, and then design an advert for the car.

➡ Students could do a survey to find out how people think that they could do something to reduce carbon dioxide emissions, or the effects of the emissions, for example they might plant a tree.

Answers to homework questions

1 **a)** Graph. **b)** It curves up on the right, showing that the amount of carbon dioxide is increasing, and the rate of increase is increasing.

2 Burning fossil fuels.

3 To get more accurate information so we can detect changes sooner.

4 They did not have much evidence to back up their claims (also, many people thought that global warming would be a good thing, or that the extra carbon dioxide would be absorbed by the oceans).

5 Suggested benefits could include: crops would grow better, we would need to use less fuel for heating, it would prevent another ice age.

6 The temperature of the Earth naturally varies a little, and the size of the changes varies a lot over the surface of the Earth. The science involved is very complicated so it is difficult to show that carbon dioxide is the cause of any warming.

7 Any sensible answer.

8 There are experts who insist that global warming is not happening. They argue that although the Earth has warmed in the most recent years, in the longer term, it is actually cooling, that computer models are unreliable because the atmosphere is so complex, and that cutting back on carbon dioxide will damage the world economy.

5 Global warming

5.1 Warming or cooling?

A Open storyboard 'Activity 5.1'. The frames show how ideas about the Earth's climate have developed. There are some questions at the bottom of each frame. Use the text/audio symbol (the blue book) to find the answers to the questions. You can use the search box at the top right of the text to look for key words. Type your answers into the bottom window in your own words, or copy and paste from the text.

B Make your storyboard more interesting by adding props to illustrate what the characters are saying, or record your own sound track to make the characters speak for themselves.

C Write a short summary of the evidence for global warming that could be used as an article in a science magazine. You can copy and paste images from Kar2ouche®, to illustrate your article.

5.2 What should we do?

A Open storyboard 'Activity 5.2'. The frames show various people discussing global warming and its effects.

There are some questions at the bottom of each frame. Use the text/audio symbol (the blue book) to find the answers to the questions. You can use the search box at the top right of the text to look for key words. Type your answers into the bottom window in your own words, or copy and paste from the text.

B Make the storyboard more interesting by making the various people explain their own ideas. You can use speech bubbles, use audio from the text provided, or even record your own sound track. You can also add props to the frames.

C Use the information you have found out to write a newspaper article that summarises global warming and what should be done about it.

5 Global warming

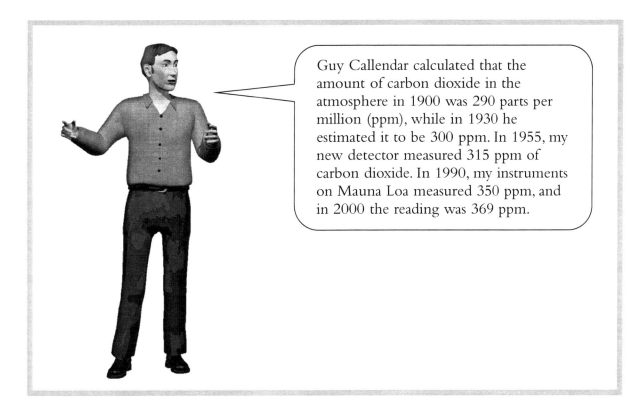

Guy Callendar calculated that the amount of carbon dioxide in the atmosphere in 1900 was 290 parts per million (ppm), while in 1930 he estimated it to be 300 ppm. In 1955, my new detector measured 315 ppm of carbon dioxide. In 1990, my instruments on Mauna Loa measured 350 ppm, and in 2000 the reading was 369 ppm.

1 a) Plot a graph of the concentration of carbon dioxide against time. You will need a sheet of graph paper.
   b) Describe the shape of your graph.
2 What is the cause of the increased amount of carbon dioxide in the atmosphere?
3 Before 1950 the amount of carbon dioxide could be measured to an accuracy of only about 10 ppm. Keeling's instruments had an accuracy of 1 ppm while now he gets measurements accurate to 0.01 ppm. Why do you think that increasing accuracy in instruments is important?
4 Most scientists now agree that the increased amount of carbon dioxide in the atmosphere is causing global warming. Why do you think Svante Arrhenius and Guy Callendar were almost ignored when they made the same claims in the early twentieth century?
5 Arrhenius thought a little global warming would be a good thing. Can you suggest any benefits of global warming?
6 Why has it been difficult to prove that global warming is taking place?
7 Imagine that you are a government advisor. Write a brief report for the minister stating why you think global warming is a problem and what you think should be done about it.

 Use books or the Internet to find out more about:

8 a) What impact global warming can have.
       OR
   b) Some of the arguments of people who do not agree that global warming is happening.

You can find some website addresses at **www.peopleinscience.co.uk**.

6 The hole in the ozone layer

Learning objectives

Students have the opportunity to learn:
- ➡ what ozone is, and how it protects us from ultraviolet radiation
- ➡ what CFCs are and why they were used
- ➡ how CFCs affect the ozone layer
- ➡ what has been done to control the use of CFCs
- ➡ the different attitudes of world governments to controlling CFCs and controlling carbon dioxide emissions.

Learning outcomes

Students:
- ➡ extract information from the text and answer questions (Activity 6.1)
- ➡ put together a 'Photostory' for a magazine (Activity 6.2)
- ➡ write an article for a magazine describing and explaining governments' approaches to CFCs and global warming (Activity 6.2).

Activity levels

Activity	KS3	KS4
6.1	Most	All
6.2	Some	Most

NC Statements

	Sc1	Sc4	BoS
KS3	1a, 1b, 1c	-	1a, 1b, 1c
KS4	1c, 1d	3f	1a, 1b, 1c

Background information

Ozone is found both high up and low down in the atmosphere. High up it forms a layer which protects the Earth from ultraviolet radiation. CFCs catalyse the breakdown of ozone and are extremely stable. Their stability means that one CFC molecule can destroy thousands of ozone molecules before it is broken down itself.

CFCs went from being wonder chemicals, making the lives of humans better, to the villains of ozone depletion in a short time. The complex chemistry of the upper atmosphere is still being discovered and Sidney Chapman is just one character involved in this part of the story. Sherwood Rowland and his colleague, Mario Molina, won a Nobel Prize for their warning of the effect of CFCs on stratospheric ozone, but this only came after the unexpected discovery of the Antarctic ozone hole by Joe Farman in the early 1980s.

Prior knowledge

It will be helpful if students know what ultraviolet radiation is, and some of its dangers. Students often confuse the greenhouse effect and ozone depletion. CFCs are greenhouse gases as well as damaging ozone but carbon dioxide has a much greater warming effect. Make sure that students know the difference between the two pollution problems.

Activity 6.1 The ozone hole 1

This activity explains what CFCs are, how they affect ozone, and what is being done about the problem. Questions are provided to help students to extract the relevant information from the text.

Activity 6.2 The ozone hole 2

This activity provides a set of headings for students to use in writing a 'Photostory' to explain the ozone hole and what is being done about it. Part C is an extension activity that asks students to write an article comparing the way governments have dealt with the CFC problem, and how they are approaching global warming. Students will find this easier if they have already done Activity 5.2, but as long as they know what global warming is, there is sufficient information in the text to provide the basis for such an article.

Characters:	Midgley, Chapman, Lovelock, Rowland, Farman, Shabalala, Simon.
Backgrounds:	Antarctic base, Midgley's Lab, Chapman's Alaska, The White House.
Props:	model of a CFC molecule, poster of ozone hole.

Lesson ideas

➡ Part C of Activity 6.2 asks students to speculate on why world governments have managed to control the use of CFCs while their action on carbon dioxide emissions has been much less effective. The answer to this lies largely with the economics of controlling emissions, and this part of the activity is probably only suitable for more able or more mature students.

➡ Hydrofluorocarbons (HFCs) are being used to replace CFCs and protect the ozone layer. The problem is that they are 1300 times more warming than carbon dioxide. HFCs are used in air conditioning systems and forecasts indicate a ten-fold increase in the use of HFCs by 2050. This could be a useful context for students to get clear in their minds the differences between global warming and ozone depletion. The advantages of HFCs are that they are not flammable and they are cheap. Students could be asked to make up their minds if they would allow them to be used or not.

➡ As a plenary activity students could be asked to take two or three clips from their completed storyboards to use as adverts for other classes. This is similar to the principal that many television programmes use 'On next week's programme ...'.

Answers to homework questions

1

1928	Thomas Midgley is asked to find a safe refrigerant. He invents the CFCs.
1931	Sidney Chapman explains the reactions forming ozone in the stratosphere.
1960s	Many thousands of tonnes of CFCs are manufactured for use in refrigerators, freezers, air conditioners, aerosols, dry cleaners and for blowing expanded plastics.
1971	James Lovelock discovers CFCs in the air over the Antarctic.
1974	Sherwood Rowland and Mario Molina discover that CFCs in the stratosphere will destroy ozone.
1984	Joe Farman publishes data that shows that the ozone over the Antarctic is being destroyed every spring.
1985	NASA realises that satellite data confirm the existence of the Antarctic ozone hole.
1987	Governments agree the Montreal protocol to restrict the use of CFCs.
1990	Governments agree to stop using CFCs by 2000.

2 It had lots of uses.

3 He could have done experiments in a laboratory and he used instruments that looked up into the stratosphere.

4 There was no evidence that what they suggested was actually happening.

5 Because the measurements that showed the problem had been ignored, so scientists thought that there was evidence that the problem was *not* happening.

6 It is much easier to stop the use of CFCs because there are alternatives, but we do not have any completely satisfactory alternatives to burning fossil fuels for energy.

7 a) It is flammable.

b) Answers may vary – students may answer that it is sensible, if the danger of the new product is less than the danger of the one it replaces, or may answer that no danger is acceptable so it is not a sensible thing to do.

c) Possible answers include not using aerosols, or doing research to find new substances that can replace CFCs or butane.

8 Air pollution also includes the problems of acid rain and smog. Most problems are caused by the burning of fossil fuels.

Ozone is formed at ground level when pollutants build up in a sunny area. It can cause respiratory problems such as triggering asthma attacks.

6 The hole in the ozone layer

6.1 The ozone hole 1

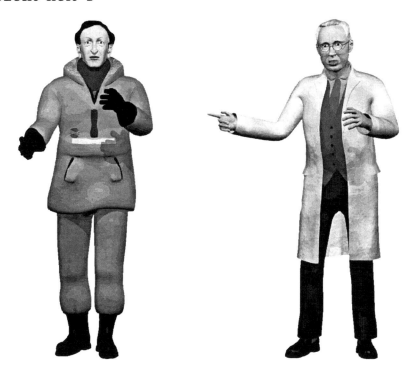

A Open storyboard 'Activity 6.1'. The frames show how scientists found out about the hole in the ozone layer, and what was done about it.

There are some questions at the bottom of each frame. Use the text/audio symbol (the blue book) to find the answers to the questions. You can use the search box at the top right of the text to look for key words. Type your answers into the bottom window in your own words, or copy and paste from the text.

B Make your storyboard more interesting by adding props to illustrate what the people are saying.

C Make speech bubbles for the characters to let them explain their own ideas, or record your own sound track.

6.2 The ozone hole 2

You can use Kar2ouche® to compose a 'Photostory' for a magazine.

A Open storyboard 'Activity 6.2'. Write a few lines to go under each heading. You can copy and paste the words of the characters, or you can write in your own words. Your report should explain the different ideas clearly.

B Add pictures to your storyboard to illustrate what you have written, then print it out. You will need to choose the right print format so that all your writing is printed.

C Write a short article for a magazine comparing the way that governments have dealt with the CFC problem, and how they are approaching the problem of global warming. Explain the reasons for the differences in the approach to the problems. You will find the text for Nande Shabalala and Ray Marlowe helpful.

6 The hole in the ozone layer

1 The table below shows some of the episodes in the story of the ozone hole. Put them in the correct order and use your own words to describe what was discovered and why it was significant.

1931	Sidney Chapman explains the reactions forming ozone in the stratosphere.
1987	Governments agree the Montreal protocol to restrict the use of CFCs.
1960s	Many thousands of tonnes of CFCs are manufactured for use in refrigerators, freezers, air conditioners, aerosols, dry cleaners and for blowing expanded plastics.
1985	NASA realises that satellite data confirm the existence of the Antarctic ozone hole.
1971	James Lovelock discovers CFCs in the air over the Antarctic.
1928	Thomas Midgley is asked to find a safe refrigerant. He invents the CFCs.
1990	Governments agree to stop using CFCs by 2000.
1974	Sherwood Rowland and Mario Molina discover that CFCs in the stratosphere will destroy ozone.
1984	Joe Farman publishes data that shows that the ozone over the Antarctic is being destroyed every spring.

2 Why was Midgley's invention so successful?
3 In the 1930s, no aircraft had flown as high as the stratosphere (15 kilometres up), so how do you think Chapman was able to work out how ozone was being formed?
4 Not a lot happened in the 1970s to stop the use of CFCs despite Rowland and Molina's warnings. Why do you think this was?
5 Why were scientists surprised by Farman's announcement, even though measurements of atmospheric ozone had been taken for years?
6 Why do you think governments have been largely successful in stopping the production and use of CFCs so that the ozone layer has a chance of recovering (slowly), but have done little to prevent global warming?
7 Other substances such as butane gas have replaced CFCs in aerosols.
   a) Why is butane more dangerous than CFCs?
   b) Do you think replacing CFCs with more dangerous substances is a wise thing to do? Explain your answer.
   c) What alternative solutions to the problem can you suggest?

 Use books or the Internet to find out more about:

8 a) Other types of air pollution.
      OR
   b) Although we need ozone in the stratosphere, when it is in the air closer to the ground it is a dangerous pollutant. Find out how ozone gets into ground level air and what effects it has.

You can find some website addresses at **www.peopleinscience.co.uk.**

H Further suggestions

This page outlines other activities that could be carried out using the text, characters and backgrounds supplied with *Earth and the Environment*.

Timeline

Ask students to use the characters to put together a timeline to illustrate how ideas about Earth and the Environment have changed over time. Each group could be asked to do one character and they could then be put together as a class display.

Characters: All except modern characters.

Making your case

Students could be asked to look at characters such as Wegener and Lovelock who tried to introduce new ideas to the scientific community. They could be asked to explain what the problem was and why their theories were eventually accepted.

kar2ouche

Quick-Start Guide

Getting Started

®

1. Adding Text

Select a piece of text and drag and drop into the caption window

Click on the orange folder to load in your own text

Type in a word and press the Search icon to find references to it within the text

Use the scroll bar to move to the relevant part of the text

Click on the blue Text and Audio tab to see and hear the full text of the library

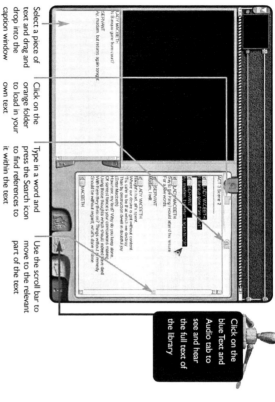

2. Adding a Background

First, click on the green Composition tab. Next, choose a background by clicking on the blue Backgrounds tab and selecting one that suits the scene you are building. It will automatically load into the Composition Window.

Click on the blue Backgrounds tab to see six backgrounds at a time. Click again to see 12 at once

The Composition Window

Click on the green arrows to toggle between selections of backgrounds

To load your own digital image as a background, click on the orange folder icon and choose an image file from your hard-disk or network drive

3. Adding Characters

To move a character, just click on it and drag it to a new location in the Composition window

To delete a character drag it into the orange waste-paper bin

Click on this green Quick Palette tab to see four characters at a time. Click again to see 16 at once

Choose characters by clicking on them and dragging and dropping them into the 'Composition' window

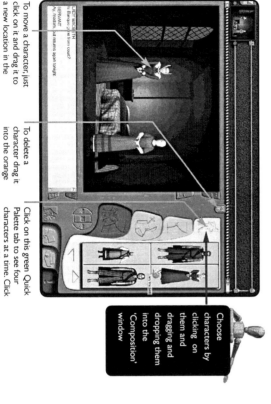

4. Adding Props

Choose from a large selection of props by clicking on the orange 'Props' tab. Drag in to the composition window

Click on the orange Props tab to see four props at a time. Click again to see 16 at once

Create copies of props by pressing Ctrl, keeping it pressed and clicking on the prop you wish to copy. Drag to a new position

Click on the green up and down arrows to move through the selection of props

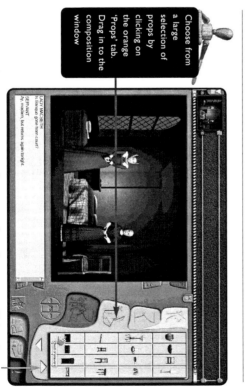
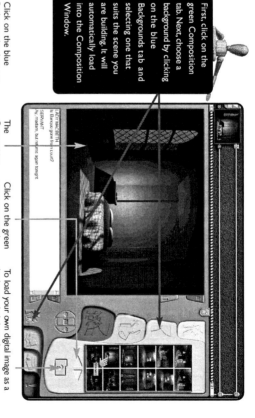

Getting Started
Quick-Start Guide

6. Building Layers

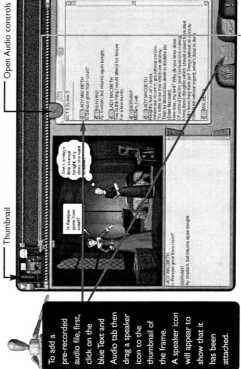

Choose the red Layers tab to move elements in the Composition Window in front or behind each other and to access the 'special effects' menu for each element in the picture.

Click on the blue tab on each layer to access its 'special effects' menu

To layer any element in front or behind another, click on its image and drag it up or down relative to other elements

LADY MACBETH
Is Banquo gone from court?
SERVANT
Ay, madam, but returns again tonight.

5. Rotate, Pose, Layer and Scale characters and props

Select the character or prop and right click to open the Manipulator.

Rotate the character or prop by clicking on the left or right arrows next to the rotate key

Pose the character or prop by clicking on the left or right arrows next to the Pose key

Change the size of the character or prop by clicking and dragging up and down on the scale key

Move the character or prop in front or behind other objects by clicking on the left or right arrows next to the Layers key

Click the large red cross to close the Manipulator

Click on the small red button to delete the character or prop

Lady Macbeth
Rotate Right

8. Adding a Pre-recorded Audio File

Open Audio controls

Thumbnail

To add a pre-recorded audio file, first, click on the blue Text and Audio tab then drag a speaker icon to the thumbnail of the frame. A speaker icon will appear to show that it has been attached.

Click on the speaker icon once to start playing the audio file and again to stop

Click on the speaker icon in the frame's thumbnail to hear the file that has been attached

7. Adding Speech and Thought Bubbles

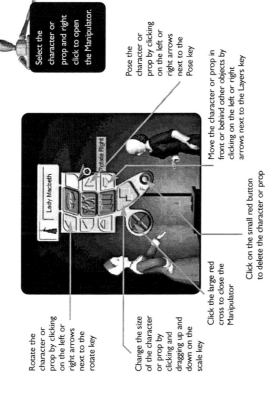

Select a character then click on the speech or thought buttons to type in what is being said or thought.

Click on the text box button to add a text box to your frame

Move a bubble by clicking and dragging the top edge of the bubble

Resize a bubble by clicking and dragging on the sides or bottom of the bubble

Move the pointer by clicking and dragging

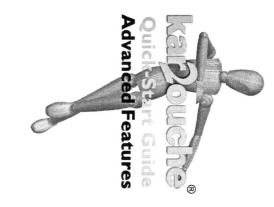

Advanced Features

9. Playing the Frame

Click on the orange Presentation tab to access the Presentation screen.

Click the Play button to see your frame shown in the presentation window. Any attached audio files will be played back.

Click on the Cycle icon for continuous looping playback

Stop or pause the frame during play back by clicking on the stop or pause buttons

Click on the Full Screen toggle button to see the frame shown as a full screen when it is played back. Click again to view play back in the Presentation Window

10. Saving and Loading Storyboards

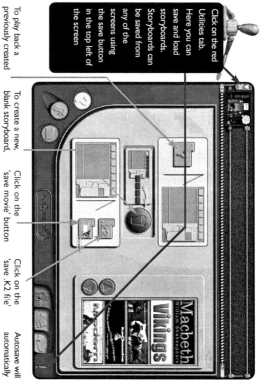

Click on the red Utilities tab. Here you can save and load storyboards. Storyboards can be saved from any of the screens using the save button in the top left of the screen

To create a new, blank storyboard, click on the New Storyboard icon

To play back a previously created story board, click on the Load button

Click on the 'save movie' button to save your storyboard as a QuickTime movie

Click on the 'save .K2 file' to save your storyboard as a Kar2ouche file

Autosave will automatically save your storyboard at set intervals

11. Printing Storyboards

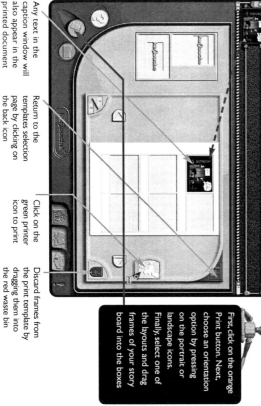

Return to the templates selection page by clicking on the back icon

Any text in the caption window will also appear in the printed document

Click on the green printer icon to print

Discard frames from the print template by dragging them into the red waste bin

First, click on the orange Print button. Next, choose an orientation option by pressing on the portrait or landscape icons. Finally, select one of the layouts and drag frames of your story board into the boxes

12. Special Effects

To access special effects, click on the green Composition tab to return to the Composition Window and click on the red Layers tab. Next, click on the blue tab associated with the element you wish to add the special effect to.

Changing the colour can help to capture the mood of the scene

Change the transparency of a character to create 'ghostly' effects

Blur the background with the sharpness setting and create a cinematic 'depth of field' effect

Scroll through the different elements using the green arrow button

Undo any special effects you have added by clicking on the reset button

QUICK-START GUIDE

kaRouche®
Quick-Start Guide
Advanced Features

14. Adding Multiple Audio Files

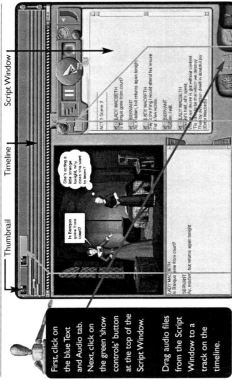

Script Window

Timeline

Thumbnail

First, click on the blue Text and Audio tab. Next, click on the green 'show controls' button at the top of the Script Window.

Drag audio files from the Script Window to a track on the timeline.

Click on the orange folder to load sound files that you have previously recorded or sound files from other sources

Show Audio controls

Click on the right edge of the thumbnail to view the duration of the frame in seconds

Change the duration of any frame by clicking and dragging on the right edge of the thumbnail

13. Adding Additional Frames

Thumbnail

Bead

To COPY your frame, drag the thumbnail of the frame to the red bead to the right of the thumbnail. A copy will be produced.

To create a BLANK frame, click on the red bead to the right of the thumbnail.

To delete a frame click on the thumbnail and drag it into the orange dustbin

When you have added more than seven frames, use the blue and yellow scroll bar to scroll through the thumbnails

16. Setting your own Options

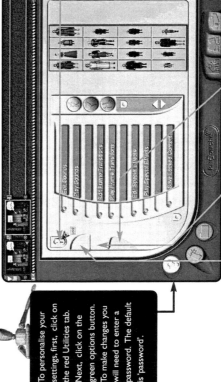

To personalise your settings, first, click on the red Utilities tab. Next, click on the green options button. To make changes you will need to enter a password. The default is 'password'.

The first options page permits changes to loading and saving files

The second options page allows specific content, sounds, transitions and text to be excluded from general access (network versions only)

The third options page controls printing and font settings

Click on the padlock to change your password

15. Recording your own Audio File

Use these controls to record your own audio files.

Click on the red microphone icon to start recording. Click on it again to finish recording. Name your sound file and it will appear as a sound bar under the frame that was selected on the Timeline

Adjust the sound levels of each track by clicking and dragging the blue volume bar up and down

To delete a sound file, select the appropriate sound bar on the Timeline and click the red 'delete' button

Click the Reset button to reset the sound file to its original length

To play back sound files choose a track (for all tracks click the blue bar, for individual tracks click on of the four track bars) and then press Play

Available September 2002

Elements and Atoms

The scientific ideas covered in *Elements and Atoms* start with ancient Greek theories about the nature of matter. The CD then looks at the work of alchemists and how they contributed to the development of the science of chemistry. The activities on the CD then cover the debate about phlogiston, Dalton's ideas about atoms, Mendeleev's development of the Periodic Table and the discovery of the structure of the atom. Students are then asked to consider the arguments for and against the use of radioactive materials in medicine.

Natural Selection and Genetics

Natural Selection and Genetics starts with Darwin's ideas about natural selection and follows the story through to the discovery of genes and DNA. The contemporary characters are used to look at the issues behind cloning, gene therapy and genetic engineering.

Earth and the Universe

Earth and the Universe looks at how and why the skies were observed in ancient times, and the different ideas people had to explain the movements of stars and planets. The development of the heliocentric solar system is covered, together with the reactions of the Christian Church to this idea. Newton's ideas on gravity are also included. The story continues through the development of optical and radio telescopes, and includes the discovery of other galaxies, pulsars and the expansion of the universe before explaining ideas about the origins of the universe. Modern characters explain recent developments such as the Hubble Space Telescope, arguments for and against spending on space technology, and the Search for Extra-Terrestrial Life (SETI).

Available March 2003

Health and Disease

Health and Disease covers a variety of topics based around the central theme. Students investigate changing ideas about heart and circulation helped by scientists such as Aristotle, Galen and William Harvey. This topic is then extended into modern heart transplants and looks at the problems faced by Christaan Barnard and his team. Students then consider the factors behind heart disease and the ethics of using animals to provide organs for transplants. Also covered is the development of ideas about the spread of disease. This includes deficiency diseases, as illustrated by the work of James Lind, the germ theory of disease, the discovery of penicillin, the development of vaccination and Edward Jenner's experiments. Students are then given information on modern medical issues such as the MMR vaccination debate, the link between smoking and lung cancer and the spread of AIDS.

Electricity and Forces

Electricity and Forces is divided up into two separate themes. It first looks at the work of Galvani and Volta amongst others. The changing ideas about forces are illustrated by the testimony of the ancient Greeks, Newton and Galileo. Radioactivity is also covered in the context of the structure of the atom. This is then extended into a modern theme with a debate about the pros and cons of using nuclear energy.

 **– explore, discover, learn**

Kar2ouche® is cross-curricular role-playing software that engages children in highly visual environments, which they can direct and experience for themselves, enabling them to produce storyboards, animations, and publications.

Kar2ouche® strongly encourages:-

- **Understanding and Interpretation**: constructing storyboards encourages closer reading and allows pupils to present their own interpretations.

- **Creativity**: using a visual environment pupils respond creatively to narrative and learn to write their own versions.

- **Critical Reflection**: by exploring multiple meanings, interpretations and consequences, pupils learn to reflect critically on their own and other's work.

- **Communication**: encouraging the communication of ideas through collaborative working and the exchange of views and presentation.

Teaching benefits include:-

- **Curriculum focussed**: Support materials for every title include lesson plans and activities mapped directly to QCA and NC requirements

- **Motivates pupils**: gets pupils absorbed in subjects they find difficult to study, saving time and boosting pupils' confidence

- **Easy to use**: pupils learn the basics with the Quick Start Guide in approximately 10 minutes

- **Versatile**: configuration options allow teachers to control the use of advanced features

- **Whole-class teaching**: Excellent for use on 'interactive whiteboards' for whole class teaching, or in ICT labs for individual or small group learning.

In addition to the series of People in Science titles outlined on the previous page, there are also **Kar2ouche**® titles available for other curriculum areas including:-

English – A series of Shakespeare plays, with **Kar2ouche**® enabling pupils to discuss key scenes in class and then explore, discover and direct the plays themselves by making their own creative multimedia presentations.

PSHE/Citizenship – A series of Kar2ouche® titles looking at issues such as Bullying, Drug Awareness and Respecting Diversity. By immersing pupils in modern, everyday situations where they can listen, discuss, then control and direct the action in a virtual role-play environment, pupils become engaged in issues that can be hard to explain and discuss.

Languages – Traditional language learning is taken to new levels of interactivity through role-play. Each Kar2ouche® languages title covers a spectrum of activities from passive listening through to practicing speaking skills and open-ended creative storytelling.

For further information on the range of **Kar2ouche**® titles please contact Immersive Education on 01865 811099, or via email at contact@kar2ouche.com. You can also visit www.kar2ouche.com for further information about **Kar2ouche**®.